The First Industrial Revolutions

THE NATURE OF INDUSTRIALIZATION

Series editors: *Peter Mathias and John A. Davis*

This series is based on papers that were originally given at the annual economic history seminars that have been sponsored since 1984 by the *Istituto Italiano di Studi Filosofici* (Naples) and held first at Oxford and then at the *Centre for Social History* in the University of Warwick.

The First Industrial Revolutions

Edited by Peter Mathias and John A. Davis

Basil Blackwell

Copyright © Basil Blackwell Ltd

First published 1989
First Published in US 1990

Basil Blackwell Ltd
108 Cowley Road, Oxford OX4 1JF, UK

Basil Blackwell, Inc.
3 Cambridge Center
Cambridge, Massachusetts 02142, USA

British Library Cataloguing in Publication Data
A CIP catalogue record for this book is available from the British Library.

Library of Congress Cataloging in Publication Data
The First industrial revolutions / edited by Peter Mathias and John A. Davis.
    p.   cm.—(The Nature of industrialization)
Includes index and bibliographical references
1. Europe—Industries—History—Congresses.   2. Industry—History-
-Congresses.   I. Mathias, Peter.   II. Davis, John Anthony.
III. Istituto italiano di studi filosofici.   IV. Series.
HC240.F46   1990
330.94′028—dc20   89–36951
                                                                     CIP

ISBN 0–631–16038–8
ISBN 0–631–16039–6 (pbk.)

Typeset in 10 on 12pt Garamond
by Wearside Tradespools, Fulwell, Sunderland
Printed in Great Britain by Camelot Press Ltd.,
Southampton

Contents

Preface

The present volume brings together the lectures that were originally given by a number of leading British economic historians in a programme organized at the University of Oxford in 1984, which was promoted by the Italian Institute for Philosophical Studies of Naples for the benefit in particular of young Italian scholars.

There is no need to elaborate on the importance of the volume, other than to say that it offers a fine example of the traditions of international cultural and scientific collaboration that are well established both in the universities of the United Kingdom and in the activities of the Italian Institute for Philosophical Studies. With the new opportunities provided by European Community projects such as ESPRIT and ERASMUS, this volume provides a stimulating example of the process of integration and collaboration that is now at work throughout European societies.

As someone who has also played a part in the realization of this Anglo-Italian initiative, with the support of the President of the Institute for Philosophical Studies Avvocato Gerardo Marrotta and the invaluable help of my colleagues Peter Mathias and John Davis, it is with the greatest pleasure that I can now wish the new series that begins with the present volume a long and successful future.

Luigi de Rosa
Istituto Universitario Navale
Napoli

Editors' Introduction

This is the first volume in a new series of studies on the process of industrialization from the eighteenth century to the present. During the last ten years there has been a remarkable renewal of interest in the origins and development of the contemporary industrial economies. As a result of new research and new ideas virtually every aspect of the ways in which we have become accustomed to understanding the process of industrialization and economic growth has come under challenge. The debate on the causes and nature of industrialization in Europe and in the wider world is now as open and as lively as it has ever been, and Professor Crafts in his contribution to the present volume goes so far as to claim that 'at last there is the prospect of research on the industrial revolution requiring a new generation of textbooks altogether.'

Whether the current rethinking of the ways in which economic history has been written in the past has as yet paved the way for a new synthesis remains open to question, and it would certainly be premature to start writing that new generation of textbooks. But in any case this is not the purpose of the present series, which is designed to provide students with a critical guide to current debates and to evaluate the significance of new research and ideas for the understanding of the process of industrialization over the last two centuries. Rather than attempt a comprehensive treatment of the process of industrialization as a whole, the volumes in the series will explore recent developments in particular fields and on particular problems.

Since much of the new work has been directed at the conventional images of the industrial revolution and the English industrial revolution in particular, this provides a natural point of departure for the series as a whole and hence the theme of its first volume. The essays that make up this volume offer a critical discussion of recent reassessments of the first industrial revolution in Britain and the relationship between industrialization in Britain and Europe in this period, as well more detailed analysis of five particular themes: financing industrialization, transport, agriculture, population and the transformation of work in European industrialization.

This thematic approach will be developed more fully in the subsequent volumes, each of which will examine a single theme or topic comparatively over the period from the eighteenth century to the present. The volumes on innovation and technology, enterprise and labour, trade and economic growth are currently in preparation and will follow shortly, while further volumes on agriculture and industrial development, urbanization, capital formation and banking are planned. Although they will be focused primarily on the European experience of industrialization over the last 250 years, each volume will also take account of Europe's changing economic relations with the rest of the world during this period.

As Professor Luigi de Rosa indicates in his preface, the original initiative for the seminars on which this series of volumes is based came from the Italian Institute for Philosophical Studies in Naples. In 1984 the Institute financed a one-week seminar in Oxford on The Industrial Revolutions in Britain and Europe, which was organized by Peter Mathias and provided the main basis for the present volume. The seminars were subsequently resumed on an annual basis at the Centre for Social History in the University of Warwick under the direction of John Davis and with the continuing support of the Institute. The success of these seminars, and the interest aroused by the papers presented at them, encouraged the editors to believe they might be welcomed as a new introduction to this broad and protean subject by a wider audience.

The annual meetings have been attended by students from Italy as well as from universities in the UK, and they have constituted an important and original initiative in European academic co-operation. While it is to be hoped that 1992 will greatly increase the opportunities for other initiatives of this sort, they are as yet still few in number. Both as editors of this series of volumes and as directors of the seminars from which they originated, we feel that it is most appropriate to take this opportunity to express our appreciation to the Institute for Philosophical Studies and its President, Avvocato Gerardo Marotta and to Professor Luigi de Rosa for their continuing support and co-operation.

Peter Mathias   John A. Davis
Downing College   Centre for Social History
Cambridge   University of Warwick

1

The Industrial Revolution: Concept and Reality

Peter Mathias

The name 'industrial revolution' is hallowed by use and it is impossible to prevent its use. Indeed it has become universalized, invoked, weekly or daily, more particularly now in relation to the second, or third, industrial revolution which we are supposedly living through ourselves – disguised sometimes as 'the upswing of the fourth Kondratief cycle'. Such claims rest upon assumptions about the first industrial revolution. Other countries have gone through their own industrial revolutions in their seasons; and there is an analogous sequence for all the industrialized nations. Equally the label has been stuck on some earlier bottles: 1540–1640 in England; the 'industrial revolution' of the thirteenth century, and even earlier sequences of change.

Is this term a misnomer? How can we identify 'the industrial revolution' as an historical phenomenon? How can we establish criteria to locate it in time and context? The term is certainly a misnomer as a metaphor insofar as it implies a single change or a changeover, as in a change of government or political regime, specific to a point in time when that discrete historical event occurred. It is also a misnomer insofar as 'revolution' implies a return to the starting point, or a finite process. The term was first used by French commentators in the 1820s, seeing an economic transformation in England as deep-rooted, structural and overwhelming in its impact as the political revolution of 1789 in France. 'Revolution' was also a term commonly used in the late eighteenth century and early nineteenth century to describe the transformations wrought in the advance of science: in the sense that Lavoisier 'revolutionized' chemistry, and so on.

It is also a misnomer insofar as it implies a sudden transformation, a high-speed change. We must examine our criteria for this metaphor in relation to the speed of change. Are they historical, judging change relative to the experience of the past; or comparative, relative to the experience of other economies and other regions at the time; or retrospective, judging against later experience, whether of Britain or other industrializing countries? We now have a longer time-span against which to judge these perspectives and also much greater knowledge, in the form of systematic quantitative data built up retrospectively by historians, to seek to make such assessments than historians even fifty years ago – let alone contemporaries living through these events. Some historians, most recently R. E. Cameron, have rejected the whole idea of an 'industrial revolution', both the term itself and what they believe it stands for as an historical process, as a violation of reality. So there is a definitional problem which is not simply a semantic issue.

The problem arises when the term is used more than tautologically or merely descriptively (giving a narrative of empirical changes), or beyond the strictly metaphorical. Designating any period as 'the industrial revolution' or the 'take-off' – or sticking any other label on the bottle – does not, of itself, specify the nature of the criteria involved. The same problem has dogged the concept of 'the Renaissance'. Any loose equation of the term with technical change or industrial innovation dissolves the problem in a methodologically indiscriminate way, by universalizing the application of it – debasing the conceptual currency – robbing it of limitation in time and context – for such piecemeal changes form a continuum in economic history, even though moving at very different rates at different epochs. As it happens the *rate* of technical change is very difficult to quantify satisfactorily even in our own day. But to speak of different rates is at once to broach the concept of some measure of overall change and comparison.

We must specify criteria and meaning if we are to locate the phenomenon in time and context. It is not until a term or concept can be identified, with criteria assessed, that it is possible to begin to test the reality of historical change in the light of the concept. It is both a conceptual and an operational problem: one has to distinguish between the definitional and conceptual identification and the narrative of empirical change deployed to describe and embody (and also to test) the assumptions contained in the concept. Conceptual identity is thus intimately involved in a potentially infinite enquiry into the facts of change and the inter-relationships of growth.

To start with, let us define the meaning of the term loosely as 'the initial phases of the long-term process of industrialization' – a process which has been continuous, even if at a varying pace and with different dynamics at

different times in different countries. Older, 'mature' industrial economies are now experiencing de-industrialization, but this comes largely
(not entirely, because the internal dynamic of change is also involved)
with the attrition resulting from successful competition by new indus-
trializers in the world economy. The process of industrialization in this
sense has been contagious, originating with Britain in the eighteenth
century.

More specifically, the two main criteria which are central to the definition
of the industrial revolution (or the onset of the process of industrialization as a sustained trend in history) are first, higher rates of growth of the
economy as a whole and second (closely linked to the first), structural
change.
Taking first the issue of higher rates of growth. If this is a main
criterion then we might hope to locate the industrial revolution in time
and space by looking for the point of discontinuity on the relevant
statistical series where that upward movement begins – the 'kink' on the
curve of the graph. Where, over the long period of centuries, the
economy has been stagnant, or growing on trend only very gradually, and
then moves into a long-term trend of higher growth rates the phasing of
that discontinuity (which does not need to be statistically identifiable at
an 'instantaneous' point in time – an actual year in the case of annually
specified time-series) offers the means of identification and location. Such
an identification is not concerned with expansion of higher rates of
growth in the very short run – on the upswing of a cyclical fluctuation or
in consequence of a sequence of good harvests – but with expansion as a
long-term trend.

But immediately the concept of higher rates of growth has to be
qualified by whether this relates to the aggregate expansion of the
economy or of expansion in terms of output per head of the population –
that is, higher rates of growth of the economic aggregate *relative* to trends
in population. 'National income per capita' is the accepted conventional
way in which relative wealth is measured between nations – a fragile
concept in many ways but the least problematical and the most generally
applicable of quantitative measures. Equally, the concept and measurement in money terms of 'rates of growth per capita' involves many
hazards, particularly in pre-twentieth-century contexts, but the concept
remains central to the analysis. This is essentially because it allows a
distinction to be made between economic expansion and economic
growth and development, which deserves elaboration. To identify both
higher rates of expansion of the aggregate and higher rates of growth in
output per head, of course, involves measuring systematically the value of

the total output of goods and services in the economy. Without such quantification no life can be breathed into the concepts. The same is true of the second concept which has to be considered, structural change in the economy.

Expansion of the economy can come by adding labour, capital, land and resources to existing modes of production, with the same sort of economic organization and with the same sort of technology. It can grow, that is to say, rather like a balloon which is being expanded but which keeps its same relative shape. In other words, the system expands without changing its nature. Economic expansion of that sort, particularly in a predominantly agricultural economy, usually occurs by extending the area of settlement and the area of cultivation at stable, or only slowly moving, levels of technique. Such a process of economic change is unlikely to give growth in the sense of rising output per capita. The productivity yielded by the technical base of the economy, the mode of production, will be the same. Indeed, if expansion continues exponentially without changing the nature of the system then diminishing returns are likely to set in with such a sequence, particularly in agriculture, because the extension of cultivation is likely to be towards less fertile land (when this occurs in a long-settled country).

Recurrent (and threatened) crises of natural resources have usually emerged in a context of exponential growth without changing the technological matrix or the resource base – whether a shortage of timber in the sixteenth century, of waterpower sites in the eighteenth century, or even oil in the late twentieth century. Of course, as shortages and pressure points develop in such a sequence of expansion, the scarcities developing in the factors of production under pressure will lead to increases in price, publicizing the scarcities and creating incentives for substitution and also for changes in the technological matrix and the resource base to overcome the constraints. Economic development may thus be encouraged in a context of economic expansion. Moreover when decisions have to be taken to increase capacity – in a context of economic expansion – the new capacity installed is likely to be of the latest available technology, and with the highest productivity, so that the average level of productivity is likely to be enhanced by the process of expansion. There would be greater inertia against taking advantage of the latest available technology if demand were not expanding and if installation of new plant could only come by dismantling existing capacity.

The argument has already led us from a consideration of economic expansion to that of economic development, which must now be considered more specifically.

Economic development implies changes in the nature of the economy which allow a cumulative increase in the efficiency of the system, a trend rise in productivity which does lift income per capita. This involves, over the long term, a change in all – or at least most of – the basic economic relationships: technological advance (incorporating techniques of higher productivity), a changing resource-base, new prime movers, new sources of energy, developing institutional structures both public and private, better organization of output and distribution, the development of a transport system, higher levels of investment to incorporate higher-productivity technology, perhaps higher capital-output ratios (all capital forms considered), the development of new financial structures and institutions to embody this, and the mobilization of a labour force. In short all main aspects of economy and society, including cultural and social values (if principally only in reaction to these developments) will be drawn into the process of economic development once it becomes sustained and cumulative.

In particular this implies structural change in the economy. The economy as it expands and increases its productivity does so by way of differential change coming to different sectors; and differential sectoral change over time produces a changed economic structure. Characteristically this means a relative fall in the share of the labour force and the share of the national output derived from agriculture. Both the economy and the labour force become more differentiated. In the late eighteenth and nineteenth centuries urbanization was integral with industrialization. This also encouraged a more differentiated institutional and economic structure with the further growth of transport and services. Throughout the eighteenth and most of the nineteenth centuries higher productivity techniques were more available in industry than in agriculture: while market demand for the products of industry was more resilient than for the products of agriculture. Thus in the twentieth century, even where in advanced countries productivity in agriculture has been rising faster than in industry, this has resulted more in a faster run-down in the agricultural labour force in those countries, than in an expansion in agricultural output relative to industrial output. Structural change is thus virtually an inevitable accompaniment to faster rates of growth and a trend rise in income per capita. Even where agriculture has remained a motor of growth in the modernization of countries in the later nineteenth and twentieth centuries – as in Denmark and New Zealand – similar institutional differentiation has occurred – with upstream industries like chemicals and engineering feeding a modernized agriculture and down-stream industries like food-processing, with all the services involved in distribution and exports, meaning that a steadily higher percentage of the labour force is to be found off the farm and in the towns and a steadily higher percentage of the national income is also contributed off the farm. There are 'demand-side' reasons for this also.

To identify a phenomenon in history, as elsewhere, one must *specify* criteria. Only when suitable criteria are specified can the industrial revolution (or the onset of the historical process of industrialization) be localized in time and society. We return to the two main criteria proposed: sustained higher rates of growth and the onset of sustained structural change in the economy. These changes of trend are to be seen in Britain in the last quarter or third of the eighteenth century. The quantitative data are not very exact; much of the economy is not covered by reliable data (particularly for output and services destined for the home market) so the conclusions must remain rough-hewn. New quantified estimates emerge annually, changing the base dates for the onset of higher rates of growth, suggesting greater or less discontinuity; a sharper or more gradual break with previous average levels, but there is consensus in all of them that, more quickly or more slowly, these new levels are attained during the eighteenth century and that cumulative structural change is identifiable after 1770–80. The next section examines the record of growth rates in more detail.

Such qualitative change was a new order which, judged in the long term – an important qualification – suggests the identification of the period 1780–1800 as that in which the foundations of a new industrial era were being laid. Possibly the differences in the consciousness of this age, that men of this generation realized they were witnessing change of a new order and a new magnitude, and felt that they could create such changes of a new order, qualitative as well as quantitative, is the best evidence of all.

The detailed record of growth

Many variants exist for the quantitative record.[1] The latest, and best tested estimates were given in the *Economic History Review* (vol. xxxvi no. 2, 1983), by N. F. R. Crafts, consolidated and extended by his book, *British Economic Growth During the Industrial Revolution* (1985). There will be other variants in the future. Their appearance does not rest upon

---

[1]   Some variants are even to be found within the same book: the assumptions of W. A. Cole in ch. 3 (on 'Demand') in R. Floud and D. McCloskey (eds), *The Economic History of Britain since 1700*, vol. 1 (1780–1860) (Cambridge, 1983), are very different from the estimates presented in ch. 1 ('The Eighteenth Century – A Survey'). Alternatives are presented by N. Harley, 'British industrialization before 1841: evidence of slower growth during the industrial revolution', *Journal of Economic History*, 42 (1982), pp. 267–89.

the production of new data alone. Lying behind estimates of changes in total national income and growth are models of the general interaction of different sectors of the economy and the growth of population. If new research produces a change in any one of these components of the model, or if new assumptions are applied to old data, then all other main relationships in the model will change. An example of this is to be found in the 'revised estimates' for 1710–40 in Floud and McCloskey (shown in column 2 of table 1). New basic research into population by Professor E. A. Wrigley and Dr R. Schofield changed the basic earlier assumption

Table 1 Growth rates (England and Wales) in the eighteenth century (average % per annum)

	1710–40	(1710–40) revised	1740–80	1780–1800	1800–31
Real output	0.2	(0.6)	1.0	2.0	3.06
Real output per head	0.2	(0.3)	0.3	1.0	1.61
Population	0.0	(0.3)	0.7	1.0	1.45
Industrial output	0.7	(0.7)	0.9	2.8	4.44
Agricultural output	0.0	(0.9)	0.5	0.6	1.64

Source: P. Deane and W. A. Cole, *British Economic Growth, 1688–1959* (Cambridge, 1962), with revision by N. F. R. Crafts and R. D. Lee, in: R. Floud and D. McCloskey (eds), *The Economic History of Britain since 1700* (Cambridge, 1981), vol. 1, p. 2.

that population growth was insignificant in the period 1680–1740. Now the assumption is that population was growing at a rate of 0.3 per cent per annum in 1710–40. Given the existing data about agricultural prices, imports and exports of agricultural products and the elasticities of demand for food (and drink), clearly, earlier assumptions about agricultural output need to be revised upwards, if production was in fact coping with an expanding population rather than a stable one. And revisions in the rate of growth of agricultural output, a major sector of the economy, clearly affect the aggregates for the economy as a whole. That is one example of what will surely be a long list of such changes within any integrated model. The uncertainties and limitations of data and great gaps in the statistical record for the eighteenth century will ensure the continuation of such changes of view.

What revisions have come from these essays in quantification? What common features are there, and what implications do they have for understanding the process of growth in eighteenth-century England? Dr Craft's new estimates (see table 2) lower the profile of economic growth that had been portrayed by Deane and Cole in 1962, and smooth the pattern of growth to some extent; finding higher rates in the first half of the century than the earlier estimates and, for the post-1780 period, rather lower rates than Deane and Cole had assessed. Note, however, the change in the sub-periods before 1780. This reduces the sharp *discontinuity* in the rates of growth pre- and post-1780, making 1780 less sharp a boundary; and sees the economy growing more gradually while industrialization is proceeding. Total annual growth rates are now assumed to be down from 2 to 1.32 per cent in the period 1700–1800; and from 3 to 2 per cent in 1800–31. When off-setting population growth, the per capita figures are even more divergent: down from 1 to 0.35 per cent in 1780–1800; and from 1.61 to 0.52 per cent in 1800–31.

The different estimates appearing in the table do possess considerable common features. There is, in all, the assumption that trends do change after 1780, that rates of growth do move upwards and stay at higher levels from that time onwards, even if more gradually than was previously assumed, and that, despite an increasing rate of growth of population, national wealth per capita was increasing on trend post-1780, in the long run, faster than had been experienced before. So, if not so specific or so sharp a frontier, the post-1780 growth rates are of a different order to the preceding trends. They also led the way to yet higher levels of growth after 1830.

Table 2   Growth rates (England and Wales) in the eighteenth century – new estimates (1982, 1985)

	1700–60	1760–80	1780–1800	1800–31
Real output	0.69	0.70	1.32	1.97
Real output per head	0.31	0.01	0.35	0.52
Population	0.38	0.69	0.97	1.45
Industrial output	0.71	1.51	2.11	3.00
Agricultural output	0.60	0.13	0.75	1.18
Cotton	1.37	5.40	9.75	5.64
Wool	0.97	0.92	0.54	1.77
Iron	0.60	3.11	5.14	4.55

Source: N. F. R. Crafts, 'British Economic Growth 1700–1831', *Economic History Review*, 36:2 (1983), pp. 177–99; and *British Economic Growth during the Industrial Revolution* (Oxford, 1985), pp. 23, 42, 45.

Behind these movements in the aggregate there are other agreed trends in the main components of the economy. Industrial output was growing faster than agriculture throughout the century and became the fastest growing sector of the economy. Within aggregate industrial output similar structural changes were taking place over time, the cotton, iron, coal, non-ferrous metal industries, growing faster than leather, beer, soap, candles and construction.[2] This is the long-known traditional story. Above all the common feature of these growth rates, compared with other countries in the early phases of their own processes of industrialization and of the industrial world as a whole (including the UK) in 1945–65 (but not after 1973), is their modesty, their gradualness. These are modest rates of growth, spread over the long time period and over the economy as a whole – agriculture as well as industry (and in important sectors industry is growing in a rural context, with some joint use of labour). Trade, transport, and the service sectors of the economy are also growing, though not as fast, so that the process of growth is widely diffused, both regionally and sectorally, leading to a more differentiated economy by way of structural change.

Why were growth rates so modest in eighteenth and early nineteenth-century Britain? And why was there no sharp discontinuity experienced in a 'take-off'? There is no single explanation. Growth was largely indigenous, based on domestic resources of all kinds, indigenous capital, indigenous skills, indigenous technology and indigenous institutions, all having to evolve in the light of evolving needs. Being the first economy, society, nation and government (central and local) to experience industrialization as a sustained and generalizing cumulative process, there were no major short cuts for Britain: no reliance upon accumulated capital from overseas to relieve any capital constraint (a constraint on speed and efficiency in mobilizing indigenous capital if not a constraint due to the shortage of savings); no shortcut to advanced technology by importing high productivity techniques already evolved overseas, for major areas of technical change. Equivalent inertia and difficulties ensured that the mobilization of a skilled, motivated, effectively deployed labour force was a long-drawn out process. The same is true with requisite institutions: a suitable legal framework for enterprise, effective company law and the like had to be built up slowly and painfully by trial and error. It was a case of learning the violin while giving the concert. Of course, this national autonomy in the process of industrialization was not absolute. A vigorous two-way traffic in ideas and formal knowledge characterized

[2]   N. F. R. Crafts, *British Economic Growth during the Industrial Revolution* (Oxford, 1985), pp. 22–3.

north-western Europe. Technology could be borrowed to a limited degree: the Jacquard loom, for example, was a technological import from France but of a very specialized nature. Certain banking and insurance skills and maritime expertise (as in cartography) were pioneered in the Netherlands. But broadly the momentum was indigenous to Britain; and the requirements to make industrialization a self-sustaining process evolved empirically, at the frontier of its evolution, within Britain.

The productivity parameters of eighteenth-century technology were also limited, compared with the later evolution of technology. Prime movers were limited in efficiency compared with later times – including the early steam engines – and in the strength and weight of materials (particularly mechanisms based on wood as a structural material). The process of growth was itself widely diffused, as has been stressed, including much expansion in industry and agriculture using traditional handicraft methods of low productivity. Few sectors were of high productivity and in the eighteenth century these were very small in relation to the total economy (e.g. cotton spinning, metal smelting) and did not exert much leverage on the national aggregates. Much symbiosis and inter-relatedness developed in the process of industrial growth between individual processes of high productivity techniques and complementary expansion of processes still dominated by handicraft techniques with low productivity (and commonly employing more labour than the high-productivity sectors). Steam-power was increasingly employed to pump out deeper mines; but the expansion of the output of coal and ores which ensued came from pick-and-shovel work. For more than half a century after 1769 the spread of high-productivity techniques using large-scale machinery and massive power in spinning yarn was associated with the growth of an army of hand-loom weavers.

Proto-industrialization

Much of the industrial advance in eighteenth-century Britain, as has been stressed, came in the form of the expansion of basically handicraft industries, with enhanced but not revolutionary artisan technology. Such a process has been named 'proto-industrialization', in a seminal article by Franklin Mendels in 1972, meaning a key apprenticeship or lead-in to industrialization proper.[3]

To merit the term, such artisan technology would need to provide the basis for a scale of handicraft production involving a degree of concentra-

---

[3]   F. F. Mendels, 'Proto-industrialization: the first phase of the industrialization process', *J. Econ. Hist.*, 32 (1972), pp. 241–61.

tion of output for more than just the local market. The concept implies a commercially orientated system of production, not just local communities being serviced by their own craftsmen in a narrow nexus of supply and demand. The form of production was characteristically the long-established 'putting-out' system with dependent artisans, working in their own households or in small workshops, being supplied with raw materials by the commercial organizers of production (if not by the merchants who eventually sold the goods in distant markets). Such a form of industrial organization characterized many sectors of the textile and para-textile industries: the making of gloves, ribbons, stockings, shoes, straw-plaiting, hat-making – as well as spinning and weaving. Dyeing, by contrast, was a process which, since medieval times, was more highly capitalized, usually an urban industry, using expensive raw materials, fuel-intensive, to a degree that had produced a structural distinction between the owners of the plant and the dependent workmen who formed, in this role, a proletariat with only their labour to sell.

Small metal wares – nails above all – with ironware such as hinges, locks, harness components, small metal-wares for ships, clocks, watches; 'toys' in brass, silver, pewter and other metal mixes, in short the whole miscellany of manufactures in the Birmingham, Sheffield and Lancashire secondary metal industries formed another main component of proto-industrial production. Such trades (particularly many of the secondary metal manufacturers) were urban-based as well as rural; but still with production based upon small workshops or domestic households. They stood in marked contrast to the more heavily capitalized, larger-scale units of production in mining and the primary metal industries, smelting and refining basic metals from ore and fuel. Even in mining, however, although unrepresentative of this sector as a whole, some output came from smallholders who divided their time between the land and digging ores, as with the small-scale lead miners of Derbyshire. Remuneration came to such workers almost always by the 'piece' rather than through a daily wage, as with the farm labourers. But they were as surely part of a capitalist system of production and trading as any wage labourers, not owning the materials upon which they worked, and in this sense an industrial proletariat had been formed long before the factory system.

Proto-industrialization contributed in several ways to industrial growth. Industrial skills were developed and a tradition of non-agricultural labour built up within a commercially orientated context at the heart of which was a money-nexus. Merchants and 'putters-out' accumulated capital and experience as entrepreneurs. A commercial infrastructure was built up in national and international markets. In the transition to large-scale technology, the organizers of production under the old system became prominent as mill owners.

In a wider context, proto-industrial development revealed important dynamic relations with demographic growth in mutual stimulus. The loom or the stocking frame, and the weekly nailing stint, became a substitute for the potato patch or the agricultural holding too small to sustain a family. Employment opportunities in these industries encouraged the establishment of new families and households, perhaps with trends toward earlier ages of marriage, without the availability of new agricultural holdings and in a context where landowners were reluctant to sub-divide farms to allow new family settlement on the land. Such industrial growth in a rural context fostered a commitment to non-agricultural employment and nurtured a non-peasant culture in the countryside. The growth of rural industries brought some integration between the agricultural and industrial labour force. In part this developed through a family or household division of labour, with wives and children helping with industrial work indoors as well as on the land. In part it followed seasonal specialization (or even day-by-day options according to the weather). During winter months when the demands made by the land were at their lowest most time could be given to the loom. In springtime, hay making and harvest the whole family was needed in the fields – at least as long as the rain allowed.

In other ways, too, it is misleading to infer that industry and agriculture have to be considered as separate entities in the eighteenth-century economy. Agricultural products provided industry with essential raw materials – wool, leather and fat (for soap-boiling and candles) being the most important – while the agricultural processing industries in milling, malting, brewing, distilling, baking, starch-making and the like took most of the cereal harvest. Equally, much of the commercial and professional activity in country market towns was activated by agricultural output, trade in agricultural products and the dealings of farmers and landowners.

At this point certain reservations about 'proto-industrialization' as an explanatory concept for the process of economic growth in eighteenth-century England should be mentioned: this was not the only source of momentum for industrial expansion. Much of the process was based in towns and cities. London was the largest industrial centre in the country. Most mining and metal-smelting was conducted on a large scale and fell outside the ambit of proto-industrialization. So also did the 'mill' industries, such as paper, which were more heavily capitalized; and 'furnace' industries such as glass. The sequence of innovations linking coal, iron and steampower proved a critically strategic path of advance in the long-term and also lay outside the ambit of the 'traditional' rural industries – although mining and metallurgy had comparably long pedigrees. Proto-industrial growth, in England as elsewhere, was not closely associated with urbanization on the production side of the process, yet urbanization had become an integral aspect of industrialization by the early nineteenth century, with profound economic effects of its own. Its effects in productivity growth were slight.

At a more conceptual level too much weight is put upon proto-industrialization when it is taken to establish a universal 'stage' in economic development, or as the critical 'hinge' between feudalism and industrial capitalism. As a historical phenomenon it is too indeterminate to serve as a universal concept of this nature. There is great indeterminacy in time: rural industries had been flourishing in England since the thirteenth century. One cannot explain the timing of industrialization in the eighteenth century from this evolution of rural industries. Great indeterminacy also exists in context. Some areas known for proto-industrial growth faded out, or were squeezed from existence by competition from other rural industries – the textile industries of the Welsh Marches and Westmorland among them.

The 'lead-in' to industrialization had other dynamics, apart from proto-industrial growth. This was also the case outside Britain. Proto-industrial growth, especially in textiles, was significant in eighteenth-century Germany and Bohemia, but did not form the critical generating force for industrialization there. Nor was proto-industrialization significant in the dynamics of growth in Scandinavian countries.

The phasing of growth in the eighteenth century

The dynamics of growth in Britain during the eighteenth century were neither simple nor unitary over the long period. In the first half of the century population was growing slowly and, from the ending of the Marlborough Wars, a secular decline soon set in with agricultural prices which lasted on trend to the mid-century. Harvests, on the whole, were bountiful and agricultural exports increased. Employment on the land and in the agricultural processing industries was maximized, as well as the disposable incomes of all non-food producers, who needed to spend a lower proportion of their money on food, because of the fall in prices. Money wage rates were maintained and translated over a rising population. Farmers' incomes (a relatively small occupational group) suffered directly from the fall in agricultural prices, through falling profits; and eventually leases would be renegotiated downwards, passing on some of the squeeze to landlords (who also had to accept rent remissions in many cases before leases fell in). Landlords also suffered from a fall in the capital value of agricultural land. But given the three-deck structure of rural society in England – landlord, tenant-farmer and agricultural labourer – falling agricultural (and food) prices were to the benefit of most labouring families in English agriculture, as well as to the many other occupational groups in English rural society servicing the agricultural community (by piece-work if not for a money wage). Falling agricultural prices thus maximized internal demand (at the base of the income pyramid) as long as money earnings were maintained, even in the countryside, as well as for all food-consumers not employed in agriculture.

Between 1710 and 1740, however, foreign trade was not a main source of momentum for industrial growth. The ratio between export values and the national income as a whole did not increase. Most increases in foreign trade took place in the export of agricultural products and in re-exports, which largely dissociated the momentum from domestic industry. Great expansion came to west coast ports, such as Bristol, Liverpool, Whitehaven and Glasgow, from the booming transatlantic commerce, but this was regional and local growth rather than a national impetus and the 'value-added' gained from re-export growth was small in comparison with indigenous industry, because of the heavy import bill associated with such exports and the relatively small extent of reprocessing and packaging involved in such basic 'colonial' goods as sugar and tobacco.

Over the two mid-century decades, 1740–60, the dynamic of growth was modified. Agricultural exports declined after their peak in 1750 and domestic agricultural prices began to move up on trend. The rate of population growth also began its steady secular increase (which continued through to the period 1811–21). Some increase in wage rates was also to be observed in the main industrializing regions, which offset the effects of the reversal in the trend of food prices after the mid-century. A boost also came to foreign trade between 1745 and the 1760s.

The following period between 1760 and 1783, again, shows some significant new directions. Foreign trade was not expanding on trend and indeed declined during the latter years of the American War of Independence, when command of the sea was lost and our main European trading partners had become military and naval antagonists. The developing conflict struck at the heart of the expansion of British international trade – transatlantic commerce. But, with the continuing increase in the rate of growth of population, wage rates in the industrializing regions now almost doubled between 1760 and the 1780s (although not in London or the south of England). Moreover, differential regional population growth was already setting a pattern for the future whereby the fastest rates of population growth were occurring in the highest-wage regions and the higher-wage sectors of the economy. As the distribution of population changed towards the Midlands and the North, therefore, internal demand was maximized. It is also the case that the *volume* of employment and total earnings (as distinct from wage *rates* in money per day or per week) would be likely to increase more than the amount suggested by the difference in wage rates between industrial employment and agriculture. Non-agricultural work probably allowed employment for more days per year than on the land, and there was a likelihood of more supplementary earnings from women and children in the expansion of industrial employment in the eighteenth century. None of these trends in the total national volume of employment and earnings are revealed from the wage-rate data. The continued stimulus for growth in the period 1760–83, evidenced by rising regional wage rates, derived principally from an internal dynamic rather than from foreign trade. 'Pressure points' were also growing in intensity from the shortage of skilled labour in industry, with a great stimulus to innovation in this period.

To the continuation of most internal trends in employment (save that of a continuing increase in wage rates) after 1783 must be added the great boost to the economy given by rapidly expanding foreign trade, which was growing by 5 per cent per annum between 1783 and 1800. Whereas, on trend, export values had remained about 11 per cent of national income between 1710 and 1780, between 1783 and 1800 they rose to *c.* 18 per cent of gross domestic product. Moreover the foreign trade 'multiplier' to industrial growth by way of the export industries was, at last, particularly strong because the increase in exports came predominantly from the industries of the 'industrial revolution' – cotton above all and woollens (both yarn and cloth), iron and metal products. A domestic investment boom is also identifiable after 1785 (encouraged by the fall in interest rates) in canals, road transport and construction. The turning points of 1783 (for foreign trade) and 1785 (for stimulus in investment projects) are both related to the aftermath of the American War of Independence. Stocks had built up in warehouses as transatlantic commerce stagnated. The opening of north European, West Indies and American markets and the sources of supply of 'colonial' goods at the end of the war produced an immediate surge of activity and peacetime trends of trade were quickly restored. Equally, wartime finance, particularly government borrowing for military expenditure, drove up interest rates and reduced investment. The 'bounce-back' from wartime constraints thus sharpened the discontinuity round the year 1783, but the following decade did see a powerful new impetus for growth which set this last period of the eighteenth century apart in several aspects of change and growth.

The section on the aggregate record of rates of growth shows that the growth of the economy as a whole did quicken, even if at a more modest incremental rate than had been previously believed. Looking beneath the aggregates one can recognize major sectoral, regional and institutional changes which give the last period of the eighteenth century (and the longer term trends which first became prominent in these years) particular significance. Improvements in the transport system – with 'interior' lines of communication being created for water carriage by the extension of canals – were on a greater scale in this period than before. The development of high-speed coaching roads also lay behind other institutional changes of great importance. The years after 1783 (continuing into the next wartime generation) saw the fastest growth in the number of country banks (which covered the country by 1800) and in the extension of banking in London. A great trend increase in the number of books and other publications took place in these years. This period also witnessed the fastest growth in the extension of shops and retailing, particularly in provincial England – notably the Midlands and the North. That was integral both with regional population trends and the faster pace of growth of urbanization in these regions. There is evidence (from banking trends and canal investment) that provincial savings were growing and being mobilized to a much greater extent, relative to London, in this phase of growth.

Critical breakthroughs in technology also occurred and began a momentous path of diffusion: rotative motion in steampower; critical advances in the iron industry (with 'puddling' and rolling processes), the development of iron machinery and advances in engineering techniques, the rapid diffusion of high-productivity techniques in cotton spinning. Because these dramatic advances affected very small sectors of the economy, as has been stressed, they did not make much impact upon the national aggregates of growth. Their impact locally and regionally was much more dramatic because the industries adopting them were often highly localized. The impact of dramatic large-scale technology – whether the cotton spinning mill, coal mine or massive London brewery – was also highly visible to visiting foreigners. The new mode of production was not representative of industrial production in 1800; nor was it in 1850. In 1800 the aggregate horsepower in windmills was possibly greater than steam-horsepower capacity, while power from watermills was still increasing in capacity and was several times greater than steam-power capacity. In 1800 perhaps half the steam-horsepower was still installed in Newcomen-type 'atmospheric' engines. Dr von Tunzelmann quantifies the incremental efficiency given to the economy by Watt-style engines (the 'social savings' resulting from the innovation) at just 0.11 per cent of gross national product in 1800.[4] This is not the final balance-sheet, of course, because steam-power was enabling industrial expansion to occur in contexts and functions for which other power sources could not provide substitutes, but the figures tell their own tale of the limited range of steam-power in the economy at the end of the eighteenth century.

Most industrial growth consisted of rural and urban workshops, not using power on a massive scale. The brewing industry offers an example of one such industrial structure: a handful of vast London 'factories' each with steam-engines, massive plant in utensils, piping, pumps, enormous storage capacity and stables for more than 100 horses. But most beer was brewed in small local urban brew-houses, without benefit of steam-power, or by village publicans selling over their own counters, or made and consumed outside the commercial market altogether by 'home brewing' in larger households, farms, and institutions. Nevertheless the new technology, with the new scale of output from the single plant, was symbolic of change from the past and herald also of the future, bringing in a new world of relationships. Levels of productivity and the possibilities of new levels of wealth stood to be transformed, as did new levels of work discipline and the context of work relative to family and household, with much else besides. The consciousness of the nation was certainly being transformed as the eighteenth century closed, as was consciousness about Britain in the eyes of Europe. And, it seems, the 'economic distance' with the 'technological gap' between Britain and Europe was widening after 1780, in reality as well as in reputation.

Table 3 indicates that, accompanying the higher growth rates which apply to all aspects of the economy after 1780, structural change also becomes a cumulative feature of the economy after 1770. This is integrally associated with sustaining the higher rate of growth for all the reasons discussed above. It should be noted that the sectoral distribution for 1688 (based on Gregory King's observations) can only have indicative value, while it may well be that Arthur Young (the main source of the data for 1770) exaggerated the role of agriculture in the national income. If so, this would diminish the extent of the relative decline shown for the last third of the eighteenth century (the 1801 distribution being better founded). However, that structural change was in fact a continuing, cumulative process is shown by the trends continuing through the whole of the nineteenth century – and, indeed, into the twentieth.

[4]   G. N. von Tunzelmann, *Steam Power and British Industrialization to 1860* (Oxford, 1978).

Table 3 Structural change (England and Wales) in the eighteenth century (% contribution to national income, current prices)

	1688		1770		1801		1851	
Agriculture	40		45		33		20	
Manufacturing, mining, construction	21		24		24		34	
Commerce, transport	12	} 39	13	} 31	18	} 43	19	} 46
Rest (government professions, domestic service etc.)	27		18		25		27	

The most prominent feature of such structural change was the decline in the relative share which agricultural output contributed to the national income and agricultural employment to the total labour force. By the end of the nineteenth century 'value added' in agriculture was down to 6 per cent of GDP and only 12 per cent of the occupied population of the United Kingdom were in the primary sector (9 per cent only in Great Britain, when Ireland is excluded). Decline in agriculture was relative to other sectors until the 1860s rather than an absolute decline in the value of output or the numbers employed. In such absolute terms agriculture continued to expand for almost a century after 1770, although the labour force increased only slowly and output at a much smaller pace than in other sectors of the economy.

Structural change centring upon the relative decline of agriculture was not just a consequence of the expansion of industry but concerned the greater differentiation and articulation of the economy and the occupational structure, as table 3 indicates, with the 'tertiary' sector of the economy (contributing services of all kinds) growing even faster than the 'secondary' sector of manufacturing, mining and construction in the last quarter of the eighteenth century, if the data can be trusted. Not all the expansion of services can be identified with direct inputs of activities supporting economic growth and the expansion of industry (and agriculture) – domestic servants increased in number; so did numbers in the armed forces during the long French wars between 1793 and 1815 – but the expansion in the contribution of commerce and transport did embody the developing financial system, the extension of canals and road services, the growing infrastructure in ports and shipping activities required to service industrial expansion.

Structural change became integral with higher growth rates because industrial output was growing more than twice as fast as agriculture in the second half of the eighteenth century. In the context of the times extra labour recruited to industrial and service occupations, at the margin, would produce a relatively greater output than if the same amount of labour had entered agricultural employment. Faster growth and structural change are therefore likely to have been associated with higher productivity in industry, and certain services associated with industrial expansion, than in agriculture. However, the growth in productivity in the economy as a whole was slow, and much of the expansion in the secondary sector was in low-productivity forms of output, as is discussed below. Hence, differences in productivity *within* each main sector in the eighteenth and early nineteenth centuries are probably more significant than average differences in productivity *between* main sectors, so that more important gains in the advance in productivity occurred by *intrasectoral* improvements than by *intersectoral* changes boosted by structural change. Structural change may well not have been, by itself, as important a boost to productivity during the industrial revolution decades in Britain as in other contexts where productivity levels in agriculture were extremely low in average terms and close to zero in marginal terms.

The sources of productivity enhancement within main sectors which typified advance were shifts from marginal peasants or smallholders on plots too small to keep their occupiers active for many months of the year, to increased employment for agricultural labourers on large, efficient farms; from the inefficiencies of fringe seasonal employment in the building industry to busy navvy gangs on the canals; from hand-loom weaving to operatives in the mills; from marginal peddling to full-time employment in a shop.

Such a pattern of growth, with such widely diffused sources of momentum, makes it difficult to accept the 'leading sector' analysis proposed by W. W. Rostow.[5] He argued that the main momentum for economic growth in eighteenth-century England came from 'a big push on a narrow front', being located primarily in the cotton and iron industries, whose expansion (with all the linkages involved) provided the economy with its 'motor of growth'. This conceptual identification of the momentum of growth lay behind the 'take-off', where the process of growth was assumed to be statistically identifiable in the short-run, showing much greater discontinuity at 1783 than subsequent quantitative investigations supported. Professor Rostow clothed in modern conceptual terms a long historiographical tradition assumed much more instinc-

[5]   W. W. Rostow, *The Stages of Economic Growth: A Non-Communist Manifesto* (Cambridge, 1960).

tively by the older textbooks which chronicled the famous inventions and saw the industrial revolution as the story of cotton, iron and the steam engine.

The main difficulty standing in the way of this hypothesis lies in the smallness of the cotton industry and the iron industry in the second half of the eighteenth century. In the 1760s cotton's net contribution to the national income was less than 0.5 per cent. It was still less than 1 per cent in 1780; with the cotton and the iron industry together adding less than 3 per cent. Cotton was regionally concentrated as an industry, paying a heavy import bill for its principal raw material. Thus, in 1770, while the cotton industry added £0.6m. to GDP; wool added £7m. and leather £5m. Looking at the record incrementally over the next 30 years, of total value-added growth in industrial output of £31m., cotton – the most rapidly growing industry – contributed £8.6m., construction £6.9m., wool £3.1m., coal £1.8m. and iron £0.5m. (the last two estimates perhaps being too low). Agriculture and services, of course, were growing as well as industry (the service sector, it seems, at a faster pace than industry). The leverage exerted by the expansion of the cotton and iron industries, even at the margin, upon the national aggregates – whether by labour employed (and wages paid), by investment and profits, by inputs and outputs of all kinds – is not sufficient to explain the national experience as a whole. The economy was not being dragged forward just on the coat-tails of a single industry, however dynamic. The sources of growth were much more diffused.

The widely diffused nature of industrial growth in the eighteenth and early nineteenth centuries accounts for the slow growth in productivity which was associated with expansion. Much industrial output, as has been stressed, came from the expansion of the 'old' world of handicraft production, hand-tools and human (or animal) energy. Although this was itself subject to technical improvement – the spinning jenny is an important example of the higher output a worker could achieve with new technology within this technological matrix – the essential fact remains that the productivity parameters of this mode of industrial growth were limited. The 'new' world of power-driven, iron machinery and large plant technology – whether in cotton spinning after 1770 or in metal-smelting – did indeed offer unprecedented levels of productivity, but the sectors of output subject to these new techniques were extremely limited in this period compared with the sectors (and the expansion of the sectors) of 'handicraft technology'. This was true of agriculture, the construction industries and the service sectors of the economy even more than in manufacturing.

In consequence much economic change in the eighteenth century has to be considered under the heading of 'economic expansion' – adding more inputs of labour, capital and resources to the economy – rather than 'economic development' – the incorporation of higher productivity techniques – although these two aspects of growth were integrally connected. Professor Crafts's latest indicators suggest that a small fraction of total rates of growth of output are to be explained by improvements in 'total factor productivity'.[6] Such quantification confirms Professor M. W. Flinn's conclusion that the upward movement in annual rates of growth was based upon 'the superimposition upon a steadily growing economy of a small group of extremely dynamic sectors'.[7]

The argument has been that the sectoral distribution of economic activity and the sources of the momentum for change in the eighteenth-century economy contrived to keep rates of growth low. With manufacturing industry contributing only about a quarter of the national income at the end of the century – which was high compared with other countries – very high rates of growth of productivity would be required in industry as a whole, or in a group of 'growth' industries, to make a significant impression on the slope of the graph of GNP per capita. Within the industrial sector a high percentage of industrial expansion involved artisan-style activities in occupations not subject in this period to major transformation in technology and productivity, and the same was true for much of the expansion in activity in other sectors, agriculture, construction and services. Great expansion came to large occupational groups such as domestic servants, hand-loom weavers, carpenters, blacksmiths, cobblers, tailors, and seamstresses, bricklayers, plasterers and the like. When the percentage contribution to total output by high-productivity sectors was so limited then the onset of their higher rates of growth is not likely to be statistically identifiable on the graph of aggregate national output and productivity.

The same point carries over to the issue of discontinuity in the rate of capital investment over time (which is taken in more detail in chapter 4, 'Financing the Industrial Revolution'). Directly 'productive' investment was a small proportion of total investment, which remained dominated by domestic building. The expansion of much activity in industry also did not require extensive new fixed capitals (but was mainly shown up in

---

[6]   The figures for annual rates of growth are: 1700–60, 0.69% (TFP 0.3%); 1760–1800, 1.01% (TFP 0.2%); 1800–30, 1.97% (TFP 0.7%). From Crafts, *British Economic Growth*, p. 81. There is less certainty about productivity estimates than about most data for this period.

[7]   M. W. Flinn, *The Origins of the Industrial Revolution* (London, 1966), p. 15.

greater levels of stocks). The growth industries where new technology did require much greater investment resources for special buildings and equipment – as in cotton spinning or the primary metal industries – and where such investment was proceeding at a high rate because of the rapid rate of expansion, did not dramatically affect total rates of investment in the economy because these industries were a very small sector of the whole economy.

But all such calculations rest upon the national economy being the numerator against which percentages of the aggregate are determined: all such calculations, and the conclusions to be drawn from them, conventionally cover nation states. They are determined, that is to say, by the economic aggregates which happen to be caught within certain political frontiers. In the case of a state covering a large land-mass, such as Russia, in the eighteenth century there may be very contrasting regional economies, with a high proportion of total population and agricultural output locked up in largely self-sufficient enclaves of static technique, having little connection with other regions by way of commercial production or markets – the 'dual economy' separation. Including such regions in the aggregates against which rates of growth are calculated will, of course, reduce the performance statistically. At the same time, therefore, Russia could have the largest iron industry in Europe and be one of its least industrialized economies according to the ratio of industrial output to GNP. Prominent regional differences of this nature were characteristic of the economies of France and Italy. Including Ireland with Great Britain has the same effect to a degree; and smaller areas, such as central Wales or much of north-west Scotland raise the same issue in principle.

This means that, when considering the dynamics of growth, whether from the point of view of production or of markets, it is important to escape from the tyranny of nationally determined statistics, which can obscure reality. To understand the process of growth the focus of analysis must often concern localities and regions – whether regions within the frontiers of a nation state or regions lying across political frontiers, as Professor Pollard has stressed.[8] The arguments about 'leading sectors' will have more force in relation to Lancashire and Cheshire (but to *which districts* in Lancashire and Cheshire, it will be questioned) for the cotton industry than in relation to the national economy as a whole. Some important parameters are, of course, determined within the unit of the nation state – taxes and tariffs, legal codes, public controls of various kinds – which affect both the production and the market side of economic

[8]   S. Pollard, *Peaceful Conquest* (Oxford, 1981); and 'Industrialisation and the European economy', *Economic History Review*, XXVI (1973), pp. 636–48.

growth, but many others are not. The statistics themselves have often been the product of the activities of the state and thus predetermine their significance. Without basing performance criteria on the norm of a national economy, runs the argument, where does one stop in terms of micro- or macro-analysis? Without entering a long debate on this theme now, the issue should be noted. New insights, at least, are possible by considering the momentum for economic change within regional rather than national frameworks.

In conclusion, the concept of the 'industrial revolution' or the onset of industrialization as a cumulative, sustained process deserves a final thought. Recent debates on the phenomenon, as a concept and as a manifestation of the historical process have centred on the twin (and related) issues of rates of growth and the degree of discontinuity observable between the pre-industrial and the industrializing economy. As we have seen in the previous section, the trend of re-assessment over the last generation – at least from the publication of the first systematically quantified analysis of the eighteenth-century economy by Phyllis Deane and W. A. Cole in 1962[9] – has been to see slower growth and less of a sharp discontinuity at 1780–3. Lying behind this revaluation of aggregate growth rates are changed assumptions about the dynamics of growth and the process of growth. Within the time-perspective of the eighteenth century, therefore, a 'gradualist' interpretation, with widely diffused roots of economic change, now holds sway. However, this depends upon the time-perspective against which such generalizations are made and have significance. Judged in the very longest historical perspective – the longest of *longues durées* – those initial phases of industrialization can still be identified as a great historical turning point; one of the great staging posts of human destiny, comparable in its impact to antecedent seminal historical developments such as the domestication of animals or the beginnings of settled agriculture. Across the timespan of centuries the beginnings of industrialization are identifiable as one such mega-phenomenon.

There is even a simple quantitative test for demonstrating that the later eighteenth century was a critical zone of change of this order in the long term, if not an identifiable turning point in the very short-run. If the average rates of growth, of 2–3 per cent p.a., which were sustained on trend for the two centuries after 1780 were extrapolated back into past centuries before 1700 the economy would soon have disappeared from

[9]   P. Deane and W. A. Cole, *British Economic Growth, 1688–1959* (Cambridge, 1962).

view. Equally if the rates of growth (in aggregate and per capita) which had characterized the very long-run (1500–1750 or 1300–1750) were extrapolated forwards over the two centuries after 1780 we would all be living still in a totally different world from that we now experience. That is the justification for still seeing some significance in the term 'industrial revolution' – if we mean by this the initial phases of the process of industrialization – and identifying it as one of the 'great divides' of human history.

Recent studies (not cited in footnotes)

B. L. Anderson, 'Money and the structure of credit in the eighteenth century', *Business History* XII (1970); F. Crouzet (ed.), *Capital Formation in the Industrial Revolution* (London, 1972); J. P. P. Higgins and S. Pollard (eds), *Aspects of Capital Investment in Great Britain, 1750–1850* (London, 1971); J. Hoppit, *Risk and Failure in English Business, 1700–1800* (Cambridge, 1987); P. Hudson, *The Genesis of Industrial Capital* (Cambridge, 1986); Peter Mathias, 'Capital, credit and enterprise in the industrial revolution', in *The Transformation of England* (London, 1979); S. Pollard, *The Genesis of Modern Management* (London, 1965); 'Fixed capital in the industrial revolution in Britain', *Journal of Economic History* XXIX (1964).

2

The New Economic History and the Industrial Revolution

N. F. R. Crafts

Introduction

Many people's perceptions of the contribution of the new economic history to our understanding of the industrial revolution are based on the work presented or discussed in Floud and McCloskey.[1] The approach is that of applying the methods of social science to history and the hope is that through the use of models and statistical methods economic history is 'augmented' rather than 'diminished' (p. xiv).

In part a glance at Floud and McCloskey does give an accurate picture. It would be correct to see the number of writers using the new economic history approach on the industrial revolution as still quite small, to a considerable extent coming from North America and as having used the new methodology on a relatively limited number of problems, such that a textbook account must rely heavily on the work of traditional economic history. Indeed the pursuit of new economic history in Britain has been very much problem orientated and topics such as the performance of the late Victorian economy and unemployment in inter-war Britain have attracted a disproportionate amount of the attention of researchers in this discipline.

Nevertheless, in other ways looking at Floud and McCloskey gives a misleading impression of the by now quite substantial contribution that the new economic history has made to the economic history of the industrial revolution. In particular, the book was basically written in

---

[1] R. C. Floud and D. N. McCloskey, *The Economic History of Britain since 1700* (Cambridge, 1981), vol. 1.

1976, since when the pace of publication has increased considerably and a synthesis of the efforts of many writers has quite radically altered our notions of the pace and nature of economic growth during the industrial revolution.

At the microeconomic level important findings have been made concerning both efficiency and equity in the economy. New economic history has always been extensively interested in the measurement and explanation of productivity change. For example, in agriculture recent work has demonstrated the importance of early improvements in yields per acre,[2] has quantified the role of increasing farm size in raising productivity[3] and has placed the debunking of Ernle's notion of an 'agricultural revolution' transforming an agriculture unchanged for centuries concomitant with the industrial revolution on a sound statistical footing. In industry von Tunzelmann[4] has established the very limited importance of steam-power in early industrialization and Hyde, in a major study of the iron industry,[5] has shown the significance both of *continuing* improvements in technology and of economic factors in the adoption and diffusion of technical improvements. Important progress has also been made in understanding the relationship of labour abundance or scarcity to technical change and thus towards resolving the debate started by Habakkuk.[6] Field[7] has demonstrated that in general Britain was a much more capital intensive economy than the United States, while James and Skinner have explained the prevalence of capital intensive methods in a particular small subset of American manufacturing (which much intrigued European visitors) by the complementarity in those activities of cheap agricultural inputs and capital.[8]

[2] M. Overton, 'Estimating crop yields from probate inventories: an example from East Anglia, 1585–1735', *Journal of Economic History*, 39 (1979), pp. 363–78; R. C. Allen, 'Inferring Yields from Probate Inventories', *J. Econ. Hist.*, 48 (1988), pp. 117–25.

[3] R. C. Allen, 'The growth of labor productivity in Early Modern English agriculture', *Explorations in Economic History*, 25 (1988), pp. 117–46.

[4] G. N. von Tunzelmann, *Steam Power and British Industrialization to 1860* (Oxford, 1978).

[5] C. K. Hyde, *Technological Change and the British Iron Industry, 1700–1870* (Princeton, 1977).

[6] H. J. Habbakuk, *American and British Technology in the Nineteenth Century* (Cambridge, 1962).

[7] A. J. Field, 'Land abundance, interest/profit rates and nineteenth century American and British technology', *J. Econ. Hist.*, 43 (1983), pp. 405–31; and 'On the unimportance of machinery', *Explor. in Econ. Hist.*, 22 (1985), pp. 378–401.

[8] J. A. James and J. S. Skinner, 'The resolution of the labor-scarcity paradox', *J. Econ., Hist.*, 45 (1985), pp. 513–40.

Turning to income distribution, in a series of important papers Lindert and Williamson have put forward a picture of income inequality increasing during the industrial revolution to a peak in the third quarter of the nineteenth century and then declining slowly.[9] More ambitiously, Williamson has developed a computable general equilibrium model of the nineteenth-century economy, with which he seeks to explain initially rising and later falling pay differentials between skilled and unskilled workers, as the result in particular of trends in technological progress.[10] This exercise, while fascinating, unfortunately seems to indicate some of the major failings to which critics of new economic history have drawn attention, notably inappropriate use of historical sources and unrealistic model-building, as Feinstein has pointed out.[11] The industrial revolution made apparent the need for revisions to Poor Law policy and new economic historians have pointed out the underlying economic and political issues related to the reforms of 1834 and the subsequent delay in 'tightening' of the operation of the law till the last quarter of the nineteenth century.[12]

At the macroeconomic level British economic history since Deane and Cole[13] has had a strong tradition of looking at overall long-run trends in economic development in the manner of Kuznets.[14] Comparisons of Britain with France,[15] later somewhat revised by Crafts,[16] have under-

[9]   P. H. Lindert, 'English occupations, 1670–1811', *J. Econ. Hist.*, 40 (1980), pp. 685–712; Lindert and J. G. Williamson, 'Revising England's social tables, 1688–1812', *Explor. in Econ. Hist.*, 19 (1982), pp. 385–408; and 'Reinterpreting Britain's social tables, 1688–1913', *Explor. in Econ. Hist.*, 20 (1983), pp. 94–109.

[10]   J. G. Williamson, *Did British Capitalism Breed Inequality?* (London, 1985).

[11]   C. H. Feinstein, 'The rise and fall of the Williamson Curve', *J. Econ. Hist.*, 48 (1988), pp. 699–729.

[12]   G. R. Boyer, 'An economic model of the English Poor Law circa 1780–1834', *Explor. in Econ. Hist.*, 22 (1985), pp. 129–67; and 'The old Poor Law and the agricultural labor market in southern England: an empirical analysis', *J. Econ. Hist.*, 46 (1986), pp. 113–35; M. E. MacKinnon, 'Poor Law policy, unemployment and pauperism', *Explor. in Econ. Hist.*, 23 (1986), pp. 299–336; and 'English Poor Law policy and the crusade against outrelief', *J. Econ. Hist.*, 47 (1987), pp. 603–25.

[13]   P. Deane and W. A. Cole, *British Economic Growth, 1688–1959* (Cambridge, 1962).

[14]   S. S. Kuznets, *Modern Economic Growth: Rate, Structure and Spread* (New Haven, Conn., 1966).

[15]   P. K. O'Brien and C. Keyder, *Economic Growth in Britain and France, 1780–1914* (London, 1978).

[16]   N. F. R. Crafts, 'Economic growth in France and Britain, 1830–1910: a review of the evidence', *J. Econ. Hist.*, 44 (1984), pp. 49–67.

lined the unsatisfactory nature of the generalizations in models such as
Rostow's stage theory of economic growth,[17] in revealing the quite
different paths which the two countries had followed in successfully
developing their economies and also have made clear the underestimation
of French economic performance common in the textbooks until recently. Feinstein's painstaking work[18] produced major revisions of knowledge concerning capital formation, while Harley,[19] and Crafts,[20] by
careful consideration of methods of allowing for price changes and
fundamental supply and demand relationships, have substantially improved upon previous estimates of the rate of economic growth. Most
recently, Crafts et al. have provided a sophisticated re-examination of the
periodization of changes in trend growth of industrial output.[21]

The macroeconomic situation before and during the industrial revolution was sensitive to the balance between population and resources.
Thanks to the pathbreaking research of Wrigley and Schofield,[22] discussed in detail elsewhere in this volume, we now understand the nature of
the 'Malthusian Problem' much more clearly. Major clarifications have, in
fact, been achieved by new economic historians developing models based
on Wrigley and Schofield's work, in particular by Fogel, Lee and
Olney,[23] which have shown respectively that there was a fairly well
defined relationship between nutrition and mortality change, that mortal-

[17]   W. W. Rostow, *The Stages of Economic Growth* (Cambridge, 1960).
[18]   C. H. Feinstein, 'Capital formation in Great Britain', in: P. Mathias and
M. M. Postan (eds), *Cambridge Economic History of Europe* (Cambridge, 1978),
vol. 7, part 1, pp. 28–96.
[19]   C. K. Harley, 'British industrialization before 1841: evidence of slower
growth during the industrial revolution', *J. Econ. Hist.*, 42 (1982), pp. 267–89.
[20]   N. F. R. Crafts, 'English economic growth in the eighteenth century: a
re-examination of Deane and Cole's estimates', *Economic History Review*, 29
(1976), pp. 226–35; and 'National income estimates and the British standard of
living debate: a reappraisal of 1801–1831', *Explor. in Econ. Hist.*, 17 (1980), pp.
176–88.
[21]   N. F. R. Crafts, S. J. Leybourne and T. C. Mills, 'Trends and cycles in
British industrial production, 1700–1913', *Journal of the Royal Statistical Society*,
152 (1989), series A, pp. 43–60.
[22]   E. A. Wrigley and R. S. Schofield, *The Population History of England,
1541–1871: A Reconstruction* (London, 1981).
[23]   R. W. Fogel, 'Nutrition and the decline in mortality since 1700: some
preliminary findings', in: S. L. Engerman and R. E. Gallmann (eds), *Long Term
Factors in American Economic Growth* (Chicago, 1987) pp. 439–555; R. D. Lee,
'Population homeostasis and English demographic history', *Journal of Interdisciplinary History*, 15 (1985), pp. 635–60; M. L. Olney, 'Fertility and the standard of
living in Early Modern England: in consideration of Wrigley and Schofield', *J.
Econ. Hist.*, 43 (1983), pp. 71–7.

ity changes were the prime movers in disturbing the population–resource balance and that lags between changes in living standards and changes in marriage behaviour were relatively short.

As a result of this recent research new economic history is starting to produce fundamental reinterpretations of key aspects of the industrialization process far beyond what had been achieved at the time of Floud and McCloskey. The gestation period has been considerable; for example, when Mathias and Deane[24] revised their famous textbooks first published in 1969 and 1965 respectively, they made only small changes. At last there is the prospect of research on the industrial revolution requiring a new generation of textbooks altogether.

It must be recognized that there are inevitably data limitations which will leave some uncertainty and I shall try to give some of the flavour of these problems in what follows. As Deane and Cole put it we have 'a set of hypotheses ... rather than a set of conclusions' (p. 78). Nevertheless, there appear to be some quite important implications of recent work which now require to be integrated into standard accounts of the industrialization process and new areas of debate which have arisen. I select the following for discussion on this occasion.

1 It now appears that the pattern of productivity growth was one of only slow acceleration and of improvements concentrated in relatively few sectors of the economy.

2 There is now no doubt that Britain's development path was quite different from that of the Continent; recognition of this requires a rethinking of the role of agricultural productivity growth in British industrialization.

3 Substantial progress has been made in the debate over the impact of industrialization on workers' living standards. The debate has certainly not been fully resolved, however; rather the areas of doubt have been better demarcated and the focal points of the controversy have shifted somewhat.

Recent estimates of economic growth

Before turning to these specific points for discussion it will be helpful to give a brief overview of recent research on the rate of economic growth

---

[24] P. Mathias, *The First Industrial Nation* (London, 1983); P. Deane, *The First Industrial Revolution* (Cambridge, 1979).

during the industrial revolution. Table 1 summarizes the main results which represent a synthesis of the work of many new economic historians. A full account of sources and methods can be found in Crafts.[25]

Table 1   Growth in real national output (% per annum)

a) Eighteenth century

	Agriculture	Industry	Commerce	Rent & services	Government & defence	National output	National output/ head
New estimates							
1700–60	0.60	0.71	0.69	0.38	1.91	0.69	0.31
1760–80	0.13	1.51	0.70	0.69	1.29	0.70	0.01
1780–1801	0.75	2.11	1.32	0.97	2.11	1.32	0.35
Deane and Cole's estimates							
1700–60	0.24		0.98	0.21	1.91	0.66	0.45
1760–80	0.47		0.49	0.68	1.29	0.65	−0.04
1780–1800	0.65		3.43	0.98	2.11	2.06	1.08

b) 1801–1831

Agriculture	Industry	Trade & transport	Housing	Domestic & personal	Government professional & rest	National output	National output/ head
New estimates							
1.18	3.00	2.13	1.53	1.37	1.37	1.97	0.52
Deane and Cole's estimates							
1.64	4.44	3.02	3.75	3.12	1.97	3.06	1.61

Source: N. F. R. Crafts, 'British Economic Growth, 1700–1831: A Review of the Evidence', *Econ. Hist. Review*, 36 (1983), pp. 177–99.

It is apparent that my recent estimates differ considerably from those of Deane and Cole.[26] In particular, note the following:

1 The pattern of acceleration in growth is much more gradual in the new estimates in terms both of overall national output and also industrial output.

[25]   N. F. R. Crafts, *British Economic Growth during the Industrial Revolution* (Oxford, 1985).
[26]   Deane and Cole, *British Economic Growth*.

2 The revisions give much lower estimates of levels of growth especially between 1780 and 1820 for overall output and on a sectoral basis in both industry and services.

3 The main differences arise not so much from new data but rather from improvements in the handling of existing information. As far as industrial output is concerned Harley showed that the Hoffmann index of industrial production gave far too high a weight to the (fast-growing) cotton industry and that Deane and Cole's resort to eighteenth-century trade data also gives an unreliable estimate.[27] Fortunately it is possible to reweight Hoffmann's data to obtain better estimates. For the early nineteenth century, Deane and Cole had problems in converting current price estimates of output into estimates adjusted for inflation and in the end used quite inappropriate price indices for the purpose, thus substantially overestimating growth in both industrial and services output.[28] The revised Hoff-

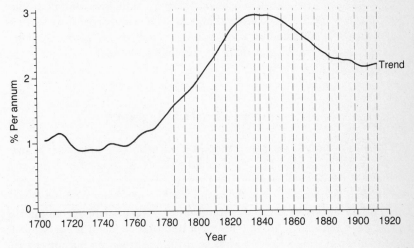

Figure 1 Trend growth in industrial production

Dotted lines denote business cycle peaks, following Aldcroft and Fearon. See the Introduction, in: D. H. Aldcroft and P. Fearon (eds), *British Economic Fluctuations, 1930–1939* (London, 1972), pp. 1–73.

Source: N. F. R. Crafts et al, 'Trends and cycles in British industrial production, 1700–1913', *Journal of the Royal Statistical Society*, 152 (1989), series A, pp. 43–60.

27 Harley, 'British industrialization before 1841'.
28 Crafts, 'National income estimates'.

mann-type index can be used to estimate industrial output growth, and for services resort to more direct measures, making greater use of employment data, is possible. 'Index number problems' of measuring growth in real output can never be ideally resolved and in truth estimates must always be of a likely range for growth rather than an exact definitive figure.

Based on a reworking of Hoffmann's index along the lines proposed by Harley, Crafts et al.[29] have estimated the trend rate of growth using a Kalman filter approach, which avoids the need to specify in advance breaks in trend, while allowing the estimated trend to be variable over time. The results, shown in figure 1, confirm the gradualness of the acceleration in trend industrial output growth implied by the new estimates and indicate that the suggestion that the 1780s saw the beginning of a take-off lasting till the end of the century[30] is likely seriously to mislead. Indeed, new economic history has generally been unsympathetic to the Rostow scheme of things, as microeconomic studies like those of von Tunzelmann and Hawke[31] do not support the notion of rapid growth dominated by a few leading sectors, and it is now clear that the rise in investment as a share of national expenditure was much less rapid than Rostow thought.[32]

The pattern of productivity growth

Revisions to output growth estimates have extremely important consequences for measured productivity growth. It is conventional in new economic history to 'account for growth' by looking at changes in the economy's productive capacity arising on the one hand from increased availability of factors of production (capital, land and labour) and on the other hand from increases in output per unit of total factor input which is obtained as a residual. As a matter of arithmetic, reduced output growth estimates lead to lower estimates of productivity growth for given growth rates of capital, land and labour. The revisions to earlier calculations called for by the new estimates of growth are shown in table 2.

The picture which now emerges is one of gradual acceleration and an

---

[29] Crafts et al., 'Trends and cycles in British industrial production'.
[30] Rostow, *The Stages of Economic Growth*.
[31] von Tunzelmann, *Steam Power and British Industry*; G. R. Hawke, *Railways and Economic Growth in England and Wales* (Oxford, 1970).
[32] Crafts, *British Economic Growth during the Industrial Revolution*, ch. 4.

Table 2 Estimates of total factor productivity growth (% per annum)

	Output growth	Due to capital	Due to labour	Due to land	TFP growth	Feinstein/ Deane & Cole TFP growth
1700–60	0.7	0.25	0.15	0.01	0.3	n.a.
1760–1800	1.0	0.35	0.4	0.05	0.2	0.2
1801–31	2.0	0.5	0.7	0.1	0.7	1.3
1831–60	2.5	0.7	0.7	0.1	1.0	0.8

Sources: my estimates are from N. F. R. Crafts, *British Economic Growth during the Industrial Revolution* (Oxford, 1985), p. 81, and the earlier estimates come from C. H. Feinstein, 'Capital accumulation and the industrial revolution', in: R. C. Floud and D. McCloskey (eds), *The Economic History of Britain since 1700* (Cambridge, 1981), vol. 1, pp. 139, 141.

elimination of the peak previously associated with 1801–31. This should not surprise us. That supposed peak was in fact a reflection of inappropriate price index numbers used to calculate real output and was implicitly assuming an inordinately rapid rate of growth of services sector output. Moreover rapid productivity growth seems most likely to occur at times of fairly high investment and it now seems to be the case that gross investment in the period 1780–1820 was little higher than in the mid-eighteenth century, at around 7–8 per cent of GDP.[33]

The downward revisions to estimates of overall productivity growth potentially have far reaching consequences for our interpretation of the locus of productivity change during the industrial revolution. The view which has been fashionable is that expressed by both McCloskey and von Tunzelmann,[34] namely that innovativeness was very widespread and that productivity advance was marked on a wide front. McCloskey establishes his conclusion by seeking to measure productivity growth in the famous, modernized sectors (cotton, woollens, iron, canals, railways, coastal shipping and agriculture) and then subtracting this figure from overall

[33]   N. F. R. Crafts, 'British economic growth, 1700–1831: a review of the evidence', *Econ. Hist. Review*, 36 (1983), pp. 177–99.
[34]   D. N. McCloskey, 'The industrial revolution: a survey', in: Floud and McCloskey, *The Economic History of Britain since 1700* (Cambridge, 1981), vol. 1, pp. 103–12; G. N. von Tunzelmann, 'Technical progress during the industrial revolution', in: Floud and McCloskey, *The Economic History of Britain since 1700*, vol. 1, pp. 143–63.

productivity growth. This leads him to suppose that the remainder of the economy accounted for 0.55 per cent of the 1.19 per cent per annum productivity growth of 1780–1860 (p. 114). This result is, however, based on the old Deane and Cole growth figures; repeating the calculation with the revised estimates gives a figure of only 0.07 per cent per annum (or about 10 per cent of the total) productivity growth accruing in the unmodernized sector.

It must be recognized, however, that available estimates of productivity growth by industry are at present very crude and it may well be that future research at the micro level will modify this picture somewhat. In this regard, it should be stressed that new economic historians insist direct measurement is important because productivity improvement was not simply the outcome of discrete, famous inventions, nor was it necessarily patented or even patentable.[35]

Nevertheless, the proposition that the transformation of production in the form of productivity advance was confined to a relatively small part of the economy coincides with similar views coming to the fore in tradition-al economic history. Musson has stressed the very limited spread of the use of steam power even in the mid-nineteenth century and the relatively unchanged nature of much small-scale traditional manufacturing.[36] Simi-larly Samuel has described in detail the continued importance of tradi-tional 'hand' technology.[37] It also helps to make sense of the recent finding that labour productivity in British industry was not significantly greater than that of France in the mid-nineteenth century, despite the much discussed 'retardation' of development in the French economy.[38] Finally the unevenness of productivity advance finds a reflection in the trade figures, which show that outside of iron and textiles only about 6 per cent of industrial output was exported in 1851.[39]

In other words, the famous inventions of the industrial revolution period should not blind us to the fact that in the mid-nineteenth century much of the economy remained small-scale, little affected by the use of steam power and characterized neither by high productivity nor compa-

---

[35]   R. C. Allen, 'Collective invention', *Journal of Economic Behaviour and Organization*, 4 (1983), pp. 1–24.

[36]   A. E. Musson, 'Industrial motive power in the United Kingdom, 1800–1870', *Econ. Hist. Review*, 29 (1976), pp. 415–39; and *The Growth of British Industry* (London, 1978).

[37]   R. Samuel, 'The workshop of the world: steam power and hand technology in mid-Victorian Britain', *History Workshop*, 3 (1977), pp. 6–72.

[38]   O'Brien and Keyder, *Economic Growth in Britain and France*; Crafts, 'Economic growth in France and Britain'.

[39]   Crafts, *British Economic Growth during the Industrial Revolution*, p. 141.

rative advantage. Equally the contributions to overall income and growth of particular inventions must not be exaggerated because of their often limited applicability and limited diffusion. Thus von Tunzelmann calculates that had the economy been forced in 1800 to do without James Watt's steam engine the cost would only have been about 0.1 per cent of national product.[40] The new economic history tends therefore to emphasize the rather limited effect of particular improvements and now also the localized nature of industrial productivity advance.

Structural change in Britain, 1688–1841

On reading the preceding account of productivity growth it must seem that the phrase 'industrial revolution' is misleading. And so in a sense it is. The phrase is not, however, to be taken literally and it implies far more than just productivity advance within industry. The key feature which has rightly been stressed in textbook accounts is, as Mathias puts it, 'the fundamental redeployment of resources away from agriculture'.[41] Thus the hallmark is the industrialization of the economy which accompanies growth, but need not imply especially rapid growth nor the same pace in the development of different economies.

In terms of structural change the new economic history has established both that 'industrial revolution' is indeed an apposite term and that British experience was markedly different from that of continental Europe. This last point was first thoroughly developed by O'Brien and Keyder, who demonstrated that France ended up as a rich country in the twentieth century by taking a quite different route from that of Britain, a route characterized by retaining a relatively large, low productivity agriculture, and who exposed the simplistic nature of much earlier work which had made damning criticisms of the French economy based on the supposition that it should have been just like Britain.[42]

The unusual nature of structural change in Britain has now been given a fuller treatment, making use of the work of many research efforts in the new economic history of Europe.[43] Something of the flavour of the results can be obtained by looking at table 3.

Table 3 compares various European countries at a similar real income

---

40   von Tunzelmann, *Steam Power and British Industry*, ch. 6.
41   Mathias, *The First Industrial Nation*, p. 2.
42   O'Brien and Keyder, *Economic Growth in Britain and France*.
43   N. F. R. Crafts, 'Patterns of development in nineteenth-century Europe', *Oxford Economic Papers*, 36 (1984), pp. 438–58.

Table 3 Nineteenth-century European economies at $550 (1970 US $)

	Urbanization	% of labour force in primary sector	% of male labour force in agriculture	% of male labour force in industry	% of income in primary sector	% of income in industry
Great Britain (1840)	48.3	25.0	28.6	47.3	24.9	31.5
Belgium (1850)	n.a.	48.9	51.4	34.4	27.0	24.0
Netherlands (1860)	n.a.	37.4	41.3	30.1	n.a.	n.a.
Denmark (1870)	25.2	47.8	48.2	22.5	49.0	20.0
France (1870)	31.1	49.3	50.6	28.7	33.5	36.0
Germany (1870)	36.1	50.0	n.a.	n.a.	39.9	29.7
Austria (1880)	n.a.	55.6	57.6	26.3	n.a.	n.a.
Norway (1890)	23.7	49.6	56.0	24.0	27.2	22.5
Hungary (1900)	n.a.	64.0	69.3	15.4	n.a.	n.a.
Sweden (1900)	21.5	53.5	53.1	24.9	27.2	30.1
Finland (1910)	n.a.	69.2	69.0	12.5	47.0	25.3
Italy (1910)	n.a.	55.4	54.2	26.5	38.2	23.9
Portugal (1910)	n.a.	57.4	61.0	21.7	n.a.	n.a.
Spain (1910)	n.a.	56.3	59.6	13.3	n.a.	n.a.

Source: N. F. R. Crafts, 'Patterns of development in nineteenth-century Europe', *Oxford Economic Papers*, 36 (1984), pp. 438–58.

level, characteristic of a country with industrialization under way. It shows Britain not only to be an early but also a very complete industrializer. At this income level Britain has a strikingly high (low) share of the labour force in industry (agriculture). Notably also Britain has virtually the same share of income and the labour force in the primary sector whereas in countries like France and Germany the share of the primary sector is much higher in the labour force than in output. It must be acknowledged that there are problems in measurement of labour force shares, particularly where workers participate in the activity of more than one sector. Further research may well refine the numbers somewhat but certainly not to the extent where the broad picture that I have described would be significantly altered.

Britain's position in 1841 represents a very considerable change from the end of the seventeenth century. The quantitative research of Lindert[44] has substantially improved our knowledge of occupational structures and it now appears that our best estimates of the share of the male labour force in industry would be 18.5 per cent in 1688, 23.8 per cent in 1759, 29.5 per cent in 1801 and 47.3 per cent in 1841. There was indeed a fundamental redeployment of resources in the economy.

From European comparisons it is clear that during 1760–1840 Britain's per capita income grew very slowly relative to that of other countries when they achieved similar income levels. On the other hand the movement of labour out of agriculture and into industry was a great deal more rapid; the average European change accompanying the income growth Britain experienced between 1760 and 1840 would have seen the share of the male labour force in industry rise only from 16.9 per cent to 25.3 per cent. A corollary of this large shift of employment, as both Bairoch and O'Brien and Keyder have calculated,[45] is that output per worker in British agriculture in 1841 was well ahead of continental standards – perhaps 60 per cent above that of France. Structural change in Britain was underpinned, it seems, by the achievement of a high level of agricultural productivity; for example, to sustain home agricultural output in 1841 with French productivity would have required 41.2 per cent of the labour force in the primary sector.[46] At the same time industrial labour productivity was perhaps only 10 per cent higher in Britain than in France.[47]

The work of new economic historians has not only revealed this somewhat paradoxical pattern of relative productivity levels but has also provided important insights to help account for it. Wrigley's careful work

---

[44]   Lindert, 'English occupations, 1670–1811'.
[45]   P. Bairoch, 'Niveaux de développement économique de 1810 à 1910', *Annales*, 20 (1965), pp. 1091–117 (see esp. p. 1096); O'Brien and Keyder, *Economic Growth in Britain and France*, p. 91.
[46]   N. F. R. Crafts, 'British economic growth during the industrial revolution: some difficulties of interpretation', *Explor. in Econ. Hist.*, 24 (1987), pp. 245–68 (see esp. p. 259).
[47]   Crafts, 'Economic growth in France and Britain.'

on the 1831 Census has confirmed that most of British 'industrial' employment was not in the new factory based activities, but rather in small scale handicraft activities.[48] Allen has shown that the traditional emphasis on the labour intensity of new crop rotations tends to ignore the impact of the move after 1700 to much larger farms with relatively high labour productivity[49] and Crafts confirms that British agriculture was dependent for most of its higher output per worker on much superior land and capital to labour ratios (characteristic of our much larger farms), rather than greater yields.[50]

The emphasis on a much better relative productivity performance in agriculture than in industry in Britain when compared with France which came from O'Brien and Keyder's work[51] might at first sight suggest that Britain had a comparative advantage in agriculture which would have tended to be antithetical to industrialization as food would be home produced and even exported. That this was not so turned on the lead developed by Britain in cotton textiles, which were so cheap to transport that we obtained virtually the whole of world trade in cotton goods.[52] Thus, British structural change was based on high productivity in agriculture and a subset of exportable manufactures rather than in industry as a whole.

Taken together with the preceding section this account of structural change now reveals the perception of 'industrial revolution' in Britain arising from research in new economic history. This view can be summarized as follows.

---

[48] E. A. Wrigley, 'Men on the land and men in the countryside: employment in agriculture in early nineteenth-century England', in: L. Bonfield, R. M. Smith and K. Wrightson (eds), *The World We Have Gained* (Oxford, 1986), pp. 295–336 (see esp. pp. 297–301).

[49] Allen, 'The growth of labor productivity'.

[50] N. F. R. Crafts, 'British industrialization in its international context', *Journal of Interdisciplinary History*, 19 (1989), pp. 415–28.

[51] O'Brien and Keyder, *Economic Growth in Britain and France*.

[52] Crafts, 'British industry in its international context'. It is a tribute to the great economist David Ricardo, to point out that he correctly identified this outcome as early as 1817, as the following passage illustrates: 'a country possessing very considerable advantages in machinery and skill, and which may therefore be enabled to manufacture commodities with much less labour than her neighbours, may in return for such commodities, import a portion of the corn required for its consumption, even if its land were more fertile and corn could be grown with less labour than in the country from which it was imported.' See p. 154 in: D. Ricardo, *On the Principles of Political Economy and Taxation* (reprinted Harmondsworth, 1971, ed. R. M. Hartwell).

1 During 1760–1840 the British economy experienced a very rapid and, by international standards, pronounced structural change. The degree of structural change was remarkable, whereas the rate of growth of per capita income was very modest, particularly before 1820.

2 'Industrial revolution' involved a fundamental redeployment of resources away from agriculture, but it did not involve pervasive rapid productivity growth and modernization throughout industry. The experience of cotton textiles is fascinating but atypical, there was no general triumph of steam power and the factory system in the early nineteenth century, nor was economic growth raised to spectacular heights by a few decisive innovations.

3 The 'industrial revolution' consisted much more of getting a lot of workers into industry than of achieving very high productivity from them once there. It is Britain's agricultural productivity, release of labour from agriculture and triumph in cotton textiles exports which emerge as truly remarkable.

The standard of living debate

New economic history has also been active in the most famous of all debates concerning the British industrial revolution, namely that over changes in the standard of living of the working classes. Here it must be said that quantitative research can only deal with part of the controversy and also perhaps supply the context within which the fate of the working classes must be considered. Progress has been made on two fronts: (a) a wider recognition of the problems involved in measuring changes in real wages; and (b) finding that the backcloth to the debate is modest growth in the early part of the industrial revolution.

Revisions to earlier views of trends in real wages have come mainly from the construction of new cost of living indices. There are still major problems with the new indices, arising from the poor quality of available budget studies and price data, but they are nonetheless distinctly superior to those provided in sources such as Phelps-Brown and Hopkins[53] which, although still widely used, must be regarded as unacceptable for use in the

[53]   E. H. Phelps-Brown and S. V. Hopkins, 'Seven centuries of the prices of consumables compared with builders' wage rates', *Economica*, 23 (1956), pp. 296–314.

standard of living debate.[54] A debate between Lindert and Williamson and Crafts, together with some reconsideration of Phelps-Brown and Hopkins work has produced a reasonable, though certainly not definitive, 'Best Guess' index.[55] The outcome of the interchange between Crafts and Lindert and Williamson is to provide a 'consensus' view of real wage growth for all blue collar workers for 1780–1850 – which is that it was virtually equal to overall personal consumption growth and modest prior to 1820 (see table 4).

Table 4 Growth of real wages and real personal consumption per head (% per year)

	Phelps-Brown and Hopkins real wages	Lindert and Williamson 1983 real wages	Crafts 1985 real wages	'Best Guess' real wages	Real personal consumption per head
1760–1800	−0.57	−0.15	n.a.	−0.17	0.25
1780–1820	−0.03	0.28	0.71	0.56	0.47
1820–1850	0.92	1.92	0.94	1.27	1.24
1780–1850	0.38	1.00	0.80	0.88	0.80

Sources: E. H. Phelps-Brown and S. V. Hopkins, 'Seven centuries of the prices of consumables compared with builders' wage rates', *Economica*, 23 (1956), pp. 296–314; P. H. Lindert and J. G. Williamson, 'English workers' living standards during the industrial revolution: a new look', *Econ. Hist. Review*, 36 (1983), table 5, using 1755–1800 for the first period; N. F. R. Crafts, 'English workers' real wages during the industrial revolution: some remaining problems', *J. Econ. Hist.*, 45 (1985), pp. 139–44, table 4. 'Best Guess' is again for Lindert and Williamson's 'all blue-collar' group of workers and uses the 'Best Guess' Cost of Living Index of Crafts in 'Real wages, inequality and economic growth in Britain, 1700–1850: a review of recent research' (Univ. of Leeds Discussion Paper, 1988), based on Lindert and Williamson's 'English workers' real wages: reply to Crafts', *J. Econ. Hist.*, 45 (1985), pp. 145–53. Real personal consumption is from Crafts, *British Economic Growth during the Industrial Revolution* (Oxford, 1985), table 5.2.

[54]   N. F. R. Crafts, 'Real wages, inequality and economic growth in Britain, 1700–1850: a review of recent research', University of Leeds Discussion Paper (1988).
[55]   P. H. Lindert and J. G. Williamson, 'English workers' living standards during the industrial revolution: a new look', *Econ. Hist. Review*, 36 (1983), pp. 1–25; and 'English workers' real wages: reply to Crafts', *J. Econ. Hist.*, 45 (1985), pp. 145–53.

It should be noted that the aggregate experience reported in table 4 subsumes quite a variety of regional trends, as might be expected in an economy with productivity growth concentrated in relatively few industries and as recent papers by Schwarz and Botham and Hunt have stressed.[56] Nevertheless, the overall impression is that real wage growth was broadly similar to the growth of national income per head, a result very different from that to which a comparison of Phelps-Brown's and Deane and Cole's work would have led.

Measurement of real wages is only part of a debate which is much wider and to a very substantial extent concerned with changes in the quality of life, where the contributions of new economic history are bound to be less than conclusive. Nevertheless it is useful to set the standard of living debate against what we now know of economic growth during the industrial revolution. Optimists such as Hartwell have always stressed the importance of substantial economic growth and rising consumption and production of manufacturing goods as rendering implausible claims of deterioration in real incomes of the working classes.[57] Table 4 shows that this argument would apply primarily to the period after 1820. In turn problems that arose during the pre-1820 period must be seen against the background of low growth in real output and productivity in an economy in which investment barely kept up with population increase.[58] Similarly it is not now difficult to reconcile slow consumption growth with what we now know about industrial output growth, especially since workers' consumption probably accounted for only about 10 per cent of industrial output in 1831 compared with perhaps 20 per cent in 1760.[59]

Even though new economic historians have for the moment arrived at a measure of agreement on overall real wage growth for blue collar workers, their research has also uncovered new areas of doubt and controversy to be considered in the next round of a never-ending debate on living standards.

---

[56] L. D. Schwarz, 'The standard of living in the long run: London, 1700–1860', *Econ. Hist. Review*, 38 (1985), pp. 28–41; F. W. Botham and E. H. Hunt, 'Wages in Britain during the industrial revolution', *Econ. Hist. Review*, 40 (1987), pp. 380–99. Contrary to the views expressed by the original authors, it is straightforward to reconcile the results in Schwarz, and Botham and Hunt, with the overall consensus view' – see Crafts, 'Real wages, inequality and economic growth'.

[57] R. M. Hartwell, 'The rising standard of living in England, 1800–1850', *Econ. Hist. Review*, 13 (1961), pp. 397–416 (see esp. pp. 398–9).

[58] Feinstein, 'Capital formation in Great Britain'.

[59] Crafts, *British Economic Growth during the Industrial Revolution*, p. 132.

Thus, Williamson, as noted earlier, has argued that the half century after the Napoleonic Wars was a period of significant increases in inequality, in which the pay of unskilled workers lagged badly behind others.[60] Unfortunately, as Feinstein has shown, this conclusion depends on a fatally flawed set of evidence on the incomes of civil servants and the model used to explain the putative surge in inequality appears to have serious failings.[61] The outcome of Feinstein's critique is that Williamson's case is very much not proven and that both better data and better models will be required to produce persuasive results.

Results have also been uncovered which do not readily fit in with the picture obtained from studying real wages and national income growth. Thus Mokyr has shown by an econometric analysis that trends in the consumption of imports such as tobacco, sugar and tea do not readily match the 'consensus view' on real wages and in fact seem to suggest very limited gains in living standards for the majority of workers till around the mid-nineteenth century.[62] Also Floud has pointed out that while the height of Army recruits was rising during the late eighteenth and early nineteenth centuries, it was falling during the second and third quarters of the nineteenth century, reflecting a less satisfactory nutritional status. Until more is known about the determinants of heights in history caution is advisable, but Floud suggests that his results may reflect deteriorations in the environment, i.e. the quality of life.[63]

Perhaps it is fair to say that new economic history has substantially enlivened and significantly improved the quality of argument in the standard of living debate, but given the quality of the data and the importance of non-quantifiable aspects of the controversy has, not surprisingly, failed to resolve it.

Concluding comments

Overall it seems fair to suggest that new economic history has already contributed a significant amount to our understanding of the industrial revolution and has certainly been much more fruitful than its critics originally expected. At the same time it must be recognized that there are

---

[60]   Williamson, *Did British Capitalism Breed Inequality?*

[61]   Feinstein, 'The rise and fall of the Williamson Curve'.

[62]   J. Mokyr, 'Is there still life in the pessimist case? Consumption during the industrial revolution, 1790–1850', *J. Econ. Hist.*, 48 (1988), pp. 69–92.

[63]   R. C. Floud, 'Standard of living and industrialisation', *Refresh*, 6 (1988), pp. 1–4.

still many important areas where relatively little has been done, for example, in exploring the economics of different types of industrial organization, in detailed sectoral studies of productivity growth or in seeking to investigate the impact of changes in the law and other institutional arrangements on economic efficiency. Finally, it must, of course, be remembered that new economic history's insights are complementary to those of other branches of economic and social history and should not be regarded as a substitute for them.

3

Industrialization in Britain and Europe before 1850: New Perspectives and Old Problems

John A. Davis

The relationship between Britain's precocious industrial revolution at the close of the eighteenth century and the subsequent industrialization of the European Continent in the course of the half century that followed has recently become the subject of major rethinking amongst economic historians. Dissatisfaction with the assumptions, models and methodologies that have guided most post-war comparative studies of European industrialization has been evident for some time, but more recently the revisionist onslaught has gained in intensity. Hardly an issue of the leading economic history journals now appears without adding some fresh contribution.[1]

Behind the attack on the old there are a variety of new approaches, each pressing claims for particular discoveries and particular new methods. There are 'new economic historians', and there are 'proto-industrial' historians; there are those who claim that the national economies are not suitable units for comparison and those who press for specialized sectoral comparisons; those who demand more counting, those who demand less.

The issues and questions that have been raised are too wide to attempt a comprehensive survey here, and this chapter will attempt only to identify the more general issues that lie behind these debates and the new research agendas, if any, for the comparative study of European industrialization down to the mid-nineteenth century that have emerged from them.

[1]   A. Milward and S. Saul, *Economic Development of Continental Europe* (London, 1973), vol. 1, pp. 30–40.

Economic history is concerned not only with explaining how, why and where industrialization occurred, but also with defining industrialization and the ways in which industrial development has been related historically to the broader processes of economic growth, social and institutional change. Debates in economic history are as much about opposing definitions of industrialization and economic growth, however, as they are about more technical questions of timing. Indeed, the most fundamental divide in economic history is still between those who see industrial development as the product, in one form or another, of market forces and of exclusively 'economic' phenomena, and those for whom industrialization either marks the consolidation of a class-based capitalist society or is the fruit of social and political as well as economic forces. There are of course many intermediary positions as well, but the divide between these two interpretations remains nonetheless fundamental. Although in recent years economic historians have tended increasingly to adopt the apparently neutral vocabulary of macroeconomic theory and quantitative analysis, the central problems of interpretation and definition have not changed.

From a more technical point of view, increased emphasis on quantitative analysis has also made the comparative study of industrial development more complex. The quantitative indices that historians now use or would like to use have grown, thereby multiplying the possible units of measurement. While this reflects a widening of empirical knowledge, it also means that what is being compared is constantly changing shape.

Even more important than the constantly changing units of measurement are the enormous gaps and uncertainties that exist in the historical data available for such comparisons. The result is that often, rather than establishing a new bedrock of empirical certainty, quantitative analysis threatens to drag comparative economic history into endless and apparently interminable wrangles over the validity of the data and the sources used.

But quantification is not the only reason why historical comparisons of national economic growth are difficult. The comparative study of European industrialization also faces problems of a more conventional kind. Each European country tends to look at its own past in a particular national perspective. Hence, for example, the study of industrialization in France has been strongly influenced by the argument that the inability of agriculture to support demographic growth over a prolonged period constituted a major 'Malthusian constraint' on France's economic development. In Germany and Italy, on the other hand, the economic consequences of political unification hold a central place in the agenda of contemporary economic historians, while for Spain the loss of the

American colonies has a similar importance.

Examples of this type could be identified for virtually every country, and obviously are not easy to accommodate in comparative studies, thereby adding to the general sense of uncertainty about what is being compared and why. Students coming for the first time to these debates may understandably feel that they have arrived in a land where most of the signposts and road-markings have been removed; for that reason alone some attempt to map out the terrain seems justified.

Europe and the 'new economic history'

The 'new economic history' offers a good starting point for examining recent development in the comparative study of European industrialization in this period, not least because the 'new economic historians' are particularly explicit in their criticism of the aims and assumptions that underpinned many earlier comparative studies.

A clear and comprehensive example of these criticisms can be found in Patrick O'Brien's recent essay on the 'typologies of European industrialization'.[2] This important and perceptive survey also indicates how much new research has been published on the economic development of individual European countries, regions and sectors in the last two or three decades. Thanks to this, our knowledge of the European economies in this period has been greatly increased, through new work on areas that were previously neglected (particularly the southern, eastern and northern 'peripheries' of the Continent) and through the revision of many conventional judgements on more familiar areas.

New and broader empirical knowledge makes many older generalizations difficult to sustain, but O'Brien rightly points out that the most important challenges to older interpretations are directed not at their empirical findings but at the methodological assumptions on which they were based. Prominent amongst these was the belief that Britain's first industrial revolution was the natural yardstick against which to measure the performance of other economies as they struggled to emulate the British lead. What began as a commonplace became a formal model, when W. W. Rostow borrowed from the vocabulary of aeronautics to transform Britain's industrial revolution into a model for all subsequent processes of industrialization, making it the empirical base for a stage theory of growth that culminated in the moment of 'take-off' into

[2]   P. K. O'Brien, 'Do we have a typology for the study of European industrialization in the 19th century?' *Journal of European Economic History*, 15:2 (1986), pp. 291–334.

sustained and irreversible economic growth.[3]

Rostow's work offered European economic historians a new agenda for comparative research. Their first task was to identify the moment of 'take-off' in each country, and then by reference to the earlier 'stages of growth' to explain the relative degree of retardation in respect to Britain. For those who found this model too mechanical and uniform, and especially for those who noted that amongst the late-comers (Russia and Italy in particular, but perhaps Germany and even France as well) industrialization was perhaps less than spontaneous, Alexander Gerschenkron provided an illuminating variant on essentially the same theme.[4] Pointing to the observable variations in the processes of industrial development in the principal European countries, Gerschenkron argued that the late-comers had the possibility of developing substitutes to make good absent prerequisites that had been present in the British industrial model. By means of state intervention or the actions of new banks, for example, they might make good the absence of capital accumulated through more spontaneous processes. Gerschenkron also suggested that late arrival might confer advantages of timing, allowing a country to jump earlier phases of industrial development that had become technologically redundant and so moving directly into the most advanced sectors of the day. But although Gerschenkron portrayed European industrialization as a varied pattern, the variations were on a single theme or 'paradigm'.

Taken together, this offered a wide agenda for research. At the centre of the agenda was the problem of 'retardation' and economic historians set out to explain why and how it was that some nations were able to close the gap, while others like Britain became (in the metaphor of David Landes[5]) short of breath and dropped back. But, as Patrick O'Brien points out, the enterprise began increasingly to lose its sense of direction and cohesion. As the empirical evidence generated by these research agendas built up, so too did the doubts over the validity of the theories that inspired them. Rather than demonstrating the validity of the concept of a sudden 'take-off', for example, research has tended to suggest that relatively slow, often lumpy and even discontinuous processes of economic development and industrialization were most generally the case.

---

[3]   W. W. Rostow, *The Stages of Economic Growth: A Non-Communist Manifesto*, (Cambridge, 1960).
[4]   A. Gerschenkron, *Economic Backwardness in Historical Perspective* (Cambridge, Mass., 1962).
[5]   D. Landes, *The Unbound Prometheus: Technological Change and Industrial Development in Western Europe from 1750 to the Present* (Cambridge, 1969); see O'Brien, 'Do we have a typology', pp. 304–23, for a detailed discussion of these points, also W. Ashworth, 'Typologies and evidence: has 19th century Europe a guide to economic growth?' *Economic History Review*, xxx (1977), pp. 140–58.

Something else has also been happening. As will be evident from other essays in this volume, the original British industrial revolution has itself been the subject of major rethinking and may well be in danger of disappearing. When the bedrock on which the comparative study of European industrialization has traditionally been premised starts to crumble, both current practices of comparative study and the analytical value of concepts like retardation are called into question.

A new agenda?

The changed image of the English industrial revolution owes much to the hard-nosed thrust of the macro-economic theories with which the 'new economic historians' have pushed aside the images of the first industrial revolution. As Professor McCloskey puts it: 'The cure for excess in metaphor is counting.'[6] On the basis of a series of new quantitative and sectoral studies, the 'new economic history' is attempting to rewrite the English industrial revolution, emphasizing the slowness and unevenness of growth, the relatively slow diffusion of steam-power and new technologies, the absence – above all – of any sudden or 'revolutionary' break with the past. In Britain – as elsewhere – it is argued, industrialization was the fruit of slow growth across a wide number of different sectors of the economy, simultaneously but over a prolonged period.

The argument that industrialization in Britain was the result of long-term growth is not in itself new, of course, and critics have suggested that the 'new economic history' has done little more than confirm what the 'old' economic history had been saying all along.[7] But

[6]   R. Floud and D. McCloskey, *The Economic History of Britain since 1700* (Cambridge, 1981), vol. 1, p. 105.
[7]   See, for example, W. Ashworth, 'The newest and truest economic history?' *Econ. Hist. Review*, xxxv (1982), pp. 434–42; also Milward and Saul, *Economic Development of Continental Europe*, p. 30; P. Mathias, *The First Industrial Nation* (London, 1983); C. Vandenbroeke, 'The regional economy of Flanders and industrial modernization in the 18th century: a discussion', *J. Europ. Econ. Hist.*, 16:1 (1987), pp. 149–70. For France, see F. Crouzet, *L'Economie Brittanique et le Blocus Continentale (1806–1813)*, 2 vols (Paris, 1958); and 'War, blockade and economic change in Europe, 1792–1815', *Journal of Economic History*, 24 (1964), pp. 567–90; and 'England and France in the 18th century: a comparative analysis of economic growth', in: R. M. Hartwell (ed.), *The Causes of the Industrial Revolution in England* (London, 1967); and 'French economic history in the 19th century reconsidered', *History* (1974); and *De la Supériorité de l'Angleterre sur la France: L'Economie et l'Imaginaire (XVIIe–VVe siècles)* (Paris, 1985). On cotton, see D. Farnie, *The English Cotton Industry and the World Market, 1815–1896* (Oxford, 1979), pp. 18–44.

leaving that aside for the moment, what are the consequences of these new interpretations of the performance of the English economy in the eighteenth and nineteenth century for the comparative study of European industrialization?

If Britain's economic performance in the era of the classical industrial revolution is now seen to have been relatively slow and patchy, and in that sense more similar to the 'European norm', it can be argued that it no longer makes sense to analyse the process of industrialization in Europe in terms of leadership and retardation. N. F. R. Crafts has rightly argued, for example, that there is no logical basis for the assumption that Britain mechanized first because the British eighteenth-century economy was in some sense superior to others. Mechanization, in other words, despite its importance becomes only one element in a broader process of growth throughout the economy as a whole. Once the identification between industrialization and economic growth is loosened in this way, the process of economic growth necessarily becomes more open-ended making it difficult, if not impossible, to establish any 'single optimal path to industrialization'.[8]

But what are we offered as an alternative basis for the comparative study of European industrialization in this period? Professor Crafts advocates the historical application of national growth accounting techniques to measure the timing of the structural changes that occurred in the different European economies as the process of industrialization progressed. These measurements can then be used to pinpoint the peculiarities present in any of these economies at a given moment. His own analysis demonstrates, for example, that in comparison with other European countries at comparable stages of development, early industrial Britain had an extremely low percentage of its population engaged in agriculture and an unusually (in comparative terms) high proportion of manufactured goods in its foreign export basket, at a time when domestic growth rates and per capita incomes were still relatively low. The reconstruction of indices across a wider range of sectors and countries would enable the economic historian, it is argued, to chart more fully over time the broad structural changes that characterized industrialization and to identify the

---

[8]   N. F. R. Crafts, 'Industrial revolution in Britain and France: some thoughts on the question "Why was England first?"' *Econ. Hist. Review*, 30 (1977), pp. 153–68. The last phrase is from P. K. O'Brien and C. Keyder, *Economic Growth in Britain and France, 1780–1914: Two Paths to the Twentieth Century* (London, 1978), p. 18.

peculiar features of each economy at a given moment.[9]

Patrick O'Brien shares a similar position when he calls for the collection of more and better data in order to proceed towards the compilation of more and more accurate national growth accounting indices. Such indices, he claims, will enable us to measure more accurately the changing levels of per capita income and consumption, of productivity and of 'any other indicators of development and relative economic efficiency which constitute the standard indicators for economists concerned with the measurement of comparative levels of development amongst the European economies since the Second World War.'[10]

That there should be more and better data series cannot be gainsaid. Indeed, many will feel that despite the econometric sophistication evident in their application the statistical base of the few comparative European studies that have so far emerged from the 'new economic history' remains fragile and speculative. The limitations of the few comparative data series that are available are widely recognized,[11] and suggest that the statistical base for this form of historical national accounting exercise is in most cases as yet largely non-existent.

If new international comparisons are to be built with something stronger than sand, there can be no doubting the need for better and broader data series. But data are a means to an end, and we must also ask how far could or might an agenda of historical analysis derived from contemporary national accounting techniques take us? Have the questions that informed the old economic history been completely disposed of or resolved? Can accounting techniques borrowed from macroeconomic theory open doors of historical understanding that were previously locked?

A case study: Britain and France

To find answers to these questions we cannot do better than turn to the

---

[9] N. F. R. Crafts, *British Economic Growth during the Industrial Revolution* (Oxford, 1985), pp. 48–52; on British agriculture see also P. K. O'Brien, 'Agriculture and the industrial revolution', *Econ. Hist. Review*, xxx (1977), pp. 175–80; E. L. Jones, 'Agriculture 1700–1780', in: R. Floud and D. McCloskey (eds), *The Economic History of Britain since 1700* (Cambridge, 1983), vol. 1, pp. 66–86.

[10] O'Brien, 'Do we have a typology', p. 331.

[11] See, for example, P. Bairoch, 'International industrial levels from 1750 to 1980', *J. Europ. Econ. Hist.*, 5:2 (1976), pp. 269–72.

recent comparative study of economic growth in Britain and France in the eighteenth and nineteenth centuries by Patrick O'Brien and Caglar Keyder.[12] In this pioneering exercise in comparative quantitative history O'Brien and Keyder up-end the old problem of why England industrialized first and France lagged behind by arguing that across the period as a whole the two economies achieved roughly comparable rates of growth.

For the eighteenth century, at least, a similar although more qualified case has been argued for some time by Francois Crouzet, but O'Brien and Keyder have sought to extend this argument to the nineteenth century as well. As a result they challenge the predominantly pessimistic school of French economic historians head-on, taking up position with units of measurement that differ from those used by earlier historians.

In place of the standard indices of industrial output and growth, they have attempted to compare the growth in per capita incomes and productivities across the economic structures of the two countries. Once the unit of measurement is changed, not only the goal posts but the game rules change as well. What is being compared is no longer industrial growth measured in terms of spindles and horsepower, but economic growth understood in much wider terms and measured primarily on the basis of per capita incomes. Secondly O'Brien and Keyder seek to emphasize the essentially contextual and relative nature of economic growth and to relate the respective economic performances of Britain and France more directly to the resources, endowments and population of the two countries.

Seen in relation to these opportunities and resources, they argue that France's performance as a whole was every bit as good as Britain's. Indeed, in some respects it was better and they suggest that France achieved sustained and long-run growth without the excesses of Coketown, with the result that the French not only found their own 'path to the twentieth century' but also a better balance between old social structures and new wealth.

Like all good iconoclasts, O'Brien and Keyder have turned a familiar image on its head and made everyone sit up and think. Their conclusions lend new weight to those who have challenged the view that French agriculture was backward and constituted an almost insurmountable obstacle to economic growth. They also reflect the work of those who have insisted that France successfully concentrated on a range of highly competitive industrial sectors, where apparent lack of interest in tech-

[12]   O'Brien and Keyder, *Economic Growth in Britain and France*.

nologies that were being adopted across the channel was not an obstacle to high labour productivity.[13]

But their study also raises major questions. In the first place, the reliability of the French statistical data on which their calculations are based is widely questioned and is generally recognized to exaggerate the rates of growth in the French economy. Secondly, their revision of the performance of French agriculture and certain sectors of manufacturing industry makes it perhaps even more difficult to understand why it was that in the key industrial sectors like steel and chemicals France remained markedly inferior, not only to Britain but also to other European and world rivals throughout the century. Thirdly, while rightly stressing that historically economic growth might follow different patterns and paths, they do not make it clear how open-ended that process was, how many different paths were possible, and to what extent effective growth could be achieved without the development of certain critical industrial sectors. Finally, their claim that France found a relatively harmonious and peaceful path to a modern economy seems to take curiously little notice of the repeated occurrences of revolution and violent tension that plagued much of French society throughout the nineteenth century.[14]

There are more general questions as well, however, that concern both the purpose of the study and the assumptions on which it is based. What, for example, is the significance of the claim that the performance of the French economy in general indicates that in the eighteenth and nineteenth centuries the French made good use of their factor endowments, available resources and prevalent demographic trends – that France, in other words, effectively exploited her 'comparative advantages'?

There is everything to be said for emphasizing the very different patterns of economic growth experienced in the European states and for

---

[13] For recent debates on French agriculture, see J. L. Goldsmith, 'The agrarian history of pre-industrial France: where do we go from here?', *J. Europ. Econ. Hist.*, 13 (1984), pp. 175–92; R. Aldritch, 'Late-comer or early starter? New views on French economic history', *J. Europ. Econ. Hist.*, 16:1 (1982), pp. 89–101; C. Heywood, 'The role of the peasantry in French industrialization 1815–1880', *Econ. Hist. Review*, xxxiv (1981), pp. 359–75; R. Roehl, 'French industrialization: a reconsideration', *Explorations in Economic History*, 13 (1976), pp. 233–81, on French technological preferences, see C. Sabel and J. Zeitlin, 'Historical alternatives to mass production: markets and technology in 19th century industrialization', *Past & Present*, 108 (1985), pp. 132–69; and esp. M. Lévy-Leboyer, 'Les processus d'industrialization: cas de l'Angleterre et de la France', *Revue Historique*, 239 (1968), pp. 281–98.
[14] For a detailed critique of O'Brien and Keyder, see esp. Crouzet, *De la Supériorité de l'Angleterre*, chs 2, 13.

drawing attention to the fact that if France at the end of the nineteenth century remained less industrialized and less urbanized than Britain, her economy had grown at a similar rate in proportion to her population and that her people enjoyed similar standards of living. But there is also a danger that if the narrower problems of industrialization are seen as unimportant in the broader context of economic development, and if we admit that there are a variety of 'paths to the twentieth century' and that there is 'no one definable optimal path to higher per capita incomes' then all may become the best in the best of all possible worlds. In both domestic and international terms industrialization becomes relatively problem-free. To argue, for example, that an economy could expand successfully by following its 'comparative advantages' implies that economic growth could be achieved without the risk of international rivalry – only identify your comparative advantage and you can grow rich and coexist happily with your neighbour. It might be argued, however, that the historical world was one of harsher realities, in which successful industrial development was perceived to be both an economic and a military prerequisite for survival. An analysis couched in terms of 'comparative advantage' would seem particularly difficult to apply in the cases of conventional 'late-comers' like Italy, Russia or Spain, where spontaneous economic growth proved difficult to achieve, but where economic modernization was seen to be a major political objective from an early stage.

This illustrates some of the difficulties that arise when 'retardation' or 'catching up' are ditched as categories of historical analysis, but the use of the theory of 'comparative advantage' raises no less important questions when it comes to the domestic economy. The theory seeks to explain how spontaneous growth engendered by the action of free market forces will follow different patterns in different economies, since each economy will exploit the comparative advantages that it enjoys with respect to its competitors (the element of competition cannot be completely eliminated).

But how, historically, are these advantages perceived and by whom? Whatever its wider strengths or weaknesses, for the theory to be operable we must assume the existence of a reasonably integrated market economy with reasonably identifiable boundaries, together with the presence of labour markets and price structures that were integrated and reasonably standardized at a national level. For most of the period considered here, arguably few of these structures obtained in France or indeed in any other European economy. Structures and markets were predominantly regional and local, labour and consumer markets were fragmented, price structures lacked uniformity, while the survival of large agricultural populations and the prevalence of domestic and artisan over factory-based production meant that wage rates showed high levels of relativity.[15]

Analysis in terms of comparative advantage therefore risks bringing into being the structures of a national economy in order to explain how a national economy came into being: a procedure in which the cart seems to have got in front of the donkey. Seen in this light it is hardly surprising that the formation of a national economy becomes relatively problem-free and harmonious. Either by the front door or the back the concept of 'comparative advantage' necessarily introduces the determinism of the invisible hand, and leaves the economic historian with little but the accounts of the past to consider.

Although the purpose is well-intentioned, it does seem to be much more difficult than might at first appear to eliminate the elements of rivalry and competition (hence also 'retardation' and 'catching-up') from the comparative study of industrialization. The case for clinging on to a single and unilinear model of industrialization based on the English experience is effectively knocked down, but that does not mean that the old agenda disappears as well. The issues that dominated the old agenda, and in particular the reasons why different economies grew at different rates at different times, why some lost ground while others were able to seize new opportunities, and why some were never able to trouble the judges at all, do not seem to have been banished by the magic wand of 'comparative advantage'.

European industrialization: integration and peaceful conquest?

If Patrick O'Brien and Caglar Keyder have argued for a process of international economic growth that was essentially conflict-free, that claim is advanced in different but even more explicit terms in a recent study by Professor Sidney Pollard. But although Pollard defines the process of industrialization in Europe as one of 'peaceful conquest', unlike O'Brien and Keyder he discards the national economies as units of analysis. Industrialization, he argues, cannot be studied through the development of national economies – these were artificial units. Econo-

---

[15]   On French labour markets and the relative nature of wage rates see, for example, M. Sonenscher, 'Work and wages in Paris in the 18th century', in: M. Berg, P. Hudson and M. Sonenscher (eds), *Manufacture in Town and Country Before the Factory* (Cambridge, 1983), pp. 147–72; also W. H. Sewell jr, *Work and Revolution in France: The Language of Labour from the Old Regime to 1848* (Cambridge, 1980).

mic growth and industrialization began as regional phenomena which occurred at roughly the same time across a wide European geography that determined Europe's future industrial landscapes. 'Large countries like Britain and France were patchwork quilts of different economic regions ... Frontiers impose a grid on this pattern ... that has relatively little influence on economic growth.'[16]

In this perspective it was the region, not the national economies, that lay at the heart of the process of industrialization: in Britain, south Lancashire, the West Riding and the Black Country; in northern Europe, the area lying between the Scheldt, the Meuse and the Rhine rivers; to the east, Silesia, Bohemia and Moravia; to the south, northern Italy and Catalonia. The building blocks of the new industrial Europe, Pollard argues, were the regional pockets of manufacturing that were already evident and established across the Continent by the mid-eighteenth century.

From these regional beginnings the broader processes of industrialization took shape and spread. Pollard insists that economic growth in nineteenth-century Europe was the fruit of the harmonious working of market forces, and takes issue with the view that European industrialization should be seen as a response to the challenge posed by Britain's precocious industrial leadership. Technologies were easily transferred, he claims, and as production and productivity expanded they generated the need for new transport networks, for credit facilities and institutions in each locality. The emergence of increasingly specialist manufacturing regions in turn encouraged agricultural specialization in others, thereby stimulating further exchange, specialization and growth. Industrialization not only grew from these regional centres but thereafter remained tied to them.

Although he discards the national economy as the unit of comparison Professor Pollard leaves little room for a variety of patterns of economic growth determined by prevailing 'comparative advantage' or for alternative paths to the twentieth century. On the contrary, he insists on the uniformity of the process of industrialization. Technology, he argues, came from Britain and was adopted lock, stock and barrel, thereby dictating the pattern and the pace of industrial development, which was replicated throughout the Continent with the same economic structures and features.

As Professor Pollard's critics have pointed out, in this perspective industrialization becomes virtually synonymous with technology trans-

[16]   S. Pollard, *Peaceful Conquest and the Industrialization of Europe, 1760–1970* (London, 1981), p. 141.

fer. But technology transfer was of course only one element amongst many in the successful development of new industries. In many cases new technologies did travel surprisingly well and fast. As well as the more familiar examples of the Cockerills, the Wilkinsons, Milne and Holker in France and the Low Countries, English machinery and English engineers found their way much further afield and the water-frame and the mule jenny were widely in use by the end of the century in the Catalan, the Bohemian and the Moravian cotton spinning industries for example. But there were also many cases where technology transfers proved far from easy, notwithstanding the presence of skilled English craftsmen and engineers.

The advantages of particular technologies also depended on a whole array of contextual conditions. The adoption of coke-smelting for iron making in Spain was quite feasible, but uneconomic owing to the high cost of fuel. The same was true in much of France and Germany in the first half of the nineteenth century. Nor does this lead to simple ledger of development and backwardness. The long dependence of French manufacturers on water-power in the first half of the nineteenth century was not a sign of technological backwardness, for example, but a function of the ready availability of cheap water power, which technological innovations like the Fourneyron hydraulic turbine made even more productive.[17]

If Pollard argues that technology determined the uniform and unilinear nature of the process of European industrialization, he sees foreign trade as the force that created a new, integrated and harmonious international economy: 'British yarn and German looms, British iron and German metal goods were added to British ships and Baltic grain and naval stores to form a symbiosis comparable to that of American cotton and Lancashire spindles.'[18]

---

[17]   See C. Fohlen, 'France 1700–1914', in: C. Cipolla (ed.), *The Fontana Economic History of Europe*, vol. 4, *The Emergence of Industrial Societies 1*, (London, 1973), pp. 7–75, esp. 48–9; Lévy-Leboyer, 'Les processus de l'industrialization', pp. 287–92; L. Bergeron, *L'Episode Napoléonien: Aspects Interieures 1799–1815* (Paris, 1972), pp. 197–207; J. R. Harris, 'Michael Alcock and the transfer of Birmingham technology to France before the revolution', *J. Europ. Econ. Hist.*, 15:1 (1986), pp. 7–58; R. Cameron, 'The economic relations of France with Central and Eastern Europe, 1800–1914', *J. Europ. Econ. Hist.*, 10:3 (1981), pp. 537–52; A. Klima, 'The beginnings of the machine-building industry in the Czech lands in the first half of the 19th century: a study in the influence of the English industrial revolution', *J. Europ. Econ. Hist.*, 4:1 (1975), pp. 49–78; J. Nadal, 'Spain 1830–1914', in: Cipolla (ed.), *The Fontana Economic History of Europe*, vol. 4, 2, pp. 537–608.
[18]   S. Pollard, 'Industrialization and the European economy', *Econ. Hist. Review*, xxvi (1973), p. 643.

That there were benefits for Britain's earlier competitors despite contemporary fears about the unequal competitiveness of British manufactures cannot be doubted. Throughout the first half of the century the net barter terms of trade were generally adverse for exporters of manufactured goods and favourable for exporters of raw materials and foodstuffs. England's new productivity in the late eighteenth and early nineteenth century was also initially limited to a relatively narrow front in ways that might directly advantage foreign competitors. Supplies of cheap British yarns stimulated the expansion and development of European weaving and finishing industries, while the growing concentration of British manufacturers on the cheaper ends of the textile markets left space for foreign competitors to exploit more specialized and higher quality markets. In this way British exports contributed to the process of international specialization and new divisions of labour: the French went for quality, while the German manufacturers looked instead for new markets in the East.[19]

Whether this triggered off a broader process of economic growth comparable to the multipliers generated by the coming together of American cotton and Lancashire spindles is another matter. Since most European countries remained protectionist throughout the period, in seeking to substitute imports they looked primarily to domestic consumer markets. But this made growth the more difficult to achieve because prolonged agrarian depression during the 1820s choked off consumer markets throughout most of Europe at precisely the moment when British exports were most aggressive (although it has to be remembered that British trade was disengaging from Europe in preference for American and Oriental markets at the same time).[20]

For all these reasons it seems doubtful whether textiles could ever bear the same load in the industrialization of the European economies that they played in England. There is little evidence, for example, that the mechanization of the Saxon cotton spinning industry created wider linkages with other sectors of the economies of the German states. The dramatic collapse of the German linen industry, until the end of the eighteenth century the single largest domestic manufacturing sector, was a direct consequence of the mechanization of cotton spinning, but may

[19] Cf. Mathias, *The First Industrial Nation*, p. 304; I. Berend and G. Ranki, 'Foreign trade and the industrialization of the European periphery in the 19th century', *J. Europ. Econ. Hist.*, 9:2 (1980), pp. 539–84; I. Glazier and V. Bandera, 'The terms of trade between Italy and the UK, 1815–1913', *J. Europ. Econ. Hist.*, 4:1 (1975), pp. 5–48.
[20] See C. Trebilcock, *The Industrialization of the Continental Powers* (London, 1981).

also have exaggerated the importance of textiles for the development of the German economies. The case of the linen industry was not typical of German manufacturing more generally. In other sectors, established organization of production, the commercial resilience of high quality craft products and the availability of cheap labour and water-power inhibited change. Historians are in broad agreement that whatever economic growth may have occurred earlier, until after 1850 most branches of manufacturing in the German states (including the heavy industries that after 1850 were to become the load-bearers of German industrialization) remained essentially artisan and pre-industrial in organization and technology. Hence the importance which German economic historians attach to railway building as the critical factor in accelerating economic growth and industrial development.[21]

The role of foreign trade in the development of the European economies in this period is also the subject of a major recent comparative study by the Hungarian historians I. Berend and G. Ranki. They too have stressed the potential advantages that the non-industrial economies might derive from trade with the more advanced countries, but paint a more differentiated picture of the immediate and longer term consequences for the weaker agrarian economies of the European periphery.[22]

Where 'weaker' economies were able to find export commodities capable of sustaining the development of secondary processing industries (the classic example being the link between wheat exports and the development of the Hungarian milling industry), Berend and Ranki argue that political and social structures were always as important as economic endowments in determing the course of economic development. Even in those cases where growth did occur, this was by no means the end of the story since success invariably brought an influx of foreign capital and capital goods, creating debts and problems of political dependence. For the weaker economies and states, it is also worth remembering that even within Europe the 'Imperialism of free-trade' could be a stark reality that brutally revealed how the disparities of political strength might well upset

[21]   K. Borchardt, 'The industrial revolution in Germany, 1830–1914', in: Cipolla (ed.), *The Fontana Economic History of Europe*, vol. 4, 1, pp. 76–160, esp. 103–4; K. Hardach, 'Some remarks on German economic historiography and its understanding of industrial relations in Germany', *J. Europ. Econ. Hist.*, 1:1 (1972), pp. 40–90, esp. 62–3; J. C. Bongaerts, 'Financing railways in the German states, 1840–60: a preliminary view', *J. Europ. Econ. Hist.*, 14:2 (1985), pp. 331–45; R. Tilly, 'German banking 1850–1914: development assistance for the strong', *J. Europ. Econ. Hist.*, 15:1 (1986), pp. 113–52.
[22]   I. Berend and G. Ranki, *The European Periphery and Industrialization, 1780–1914* (Cambridge, 1982); and 'Foreign trade and the industrialization of the European periphery'.

the neater logic of both comparative economic advantages and 'peaceful conquest'.

The region as an alternative

One of the most striking aspects of Professor Pollard's study is the central place he assigns to the region in the comparative study of European industrialization. To some extent this reflects the great boom that has taken place in recent years in local and regional economic studies in Europe, although Pollard's own analysis differs significantly both in approach and conclusion from much of the research on what has become known as 'proto-industry'.

One of the first problems is to define what did or did not constitute a region in economic terms. Geographers treat the whole question of regions with kid gloves, and economic historians have even more reason to do the same since the economic characteristics of regions change even more rapidly and radically than do their geographical features.

Some of these problems are also evident in the case of the region that lies at the heart of Pollard's analysis: the area bounded by the Scheldt–Meuse–Rhine. Although some of the earliest centres of Continental industrialization did develop within these areas, the sense in which they formed a cohesive economic region (politically they were of course fragmented in ways that constantly changed) remains far from clear. Belgian economic historians, for example, tend to stress that the area was subdivided by the Meuse and the Scheldt in ways that made internal communication difficult and encouraged the development of four separate regions (marked out by the four main coal basins – the Borinage in western Hainault, Charleroi in eastern Hainault, the central region and Liège). Each of these developed their own largely external network of contacts and markets. Annexation to France, for example, made the Borinage coal field the principal supplier of Napoleonic France (by the end of the Empire it was providing 75 per cent of France's total coal consumption). It was external contacts such as these that shaped the patterns of growth in each of these areas, and rather than forming a coherent economic region each locality developed highly differentiated and also rather hesitant ways.[23]

[23]   J. Dhont and M. Bruwier, 'The Low Countries, 1700–1914', in Cipolla (ed.), *The Fontana Economic History of Europe*, vol. 4, 1, pp. 329–66, esp. 331–6; J. Van Hutte, 'Economic development of Belgium and the Netherlands', *J. Europ. Econ. Hist.*, 1 (1972), pp. 105–19; J. Mokyr (ed.), *The Economics of the Industrial Revolution* (London, 1985).

Despite the uncertainties that surround the definition of regional economies, Professor Pollard repeatedly contrasts the natural economic space constituted by the region with the nation, which he portrays as an artificial and distorted economic unit. He argues that the attempts to divert regional economic growth into 'national' boundaries upset the early process of peaceful expansion, causing harmony to give way to rivalry, free-trade to protectionism and imperialism, unconstrained growth to increasingly unstable forms of economic development.

Such a view would seem to have a close affinity with Cobdenite liberalism, but it begs many questions. It leaves us without any clear definition of the nature of national economies and how they came into being, other than the fact that they were distortions of more spontaneous processes of growth and therefore a bad thing. Nor, on the other hand, does it explain what would have happened otherwise to regional economies that expanded successfully. At the same time, the economic fate of those regions that did not have the good fortune to experience spontaneous economic growth is passed over pretty much in silence.

A very different approach to regional economic growth can be found in the recently flourishing field of studies on European 'proto-industrialization' – a term that first gained currency thanks mainly to the work of the late F. F. Mendels, whose tragically early death has sadly deprived economic historians of a creative and generous colleague.[24] Although Mendels defined proto-industry as the 'first phase of the industrialization process', subsequent work on manufacturing in Europe before the advent of the factory system has moved away from the notion that the spread of new market-orientated rural industries in the seventeenth and eighteenth centuries constituted a necessary and preparatory phase in the process of industrialization.

Rather than the attempt to graft domestic production on to a stage theory of growth it was Mendels's concern to explore the social and institutional contexts within which new forms of production developed, and with what consequences, that has inspired a new wave of research on pre-industrial manufacturing. In Mendels's own case this meant first and foremost exploring the relationship between the expansion of rural industries and demographic growth in eighteenth-century Flanders. Subsequent studies have further developed the study of the demographic dimensions of early manufacturing, and have moved on from reconstruct-

---

[24]   F. F. Mendels, 'Proto-industrialization: the first phase of the industrialization process', *J. Econ. Hist.*, 32 (1972), pp. 241–61; and 'Des industries rurales et la protoindustrialization: histoire d'un changement de perspective', *Annales E.S.C.*, 5 (1984), pp. 977–1008.

ing the role of domestic manufactures in lowering marriage ages and increasing fertility to explore changing family structures, the changing roles of women in work, and the concept of a 'family economy'.

Recent judgements on the work that has emerged from the proto-industrial agenda still tend to be negative. It is argued that while Mendels's formulation was too narrow and too functionalist, other practitioners seem to have no common theory or agenda at all. Critics claim that despite the accumulation of localized studies no clear links between proto-industry and industrialization have been demonstrated, no explanations of why some proto-industrial regions industrialized whereas others did not have been given, key pre-industrial sectors like mining and metal-working have generally been omitted, and no generalizations have been sustained on the possible connection between the spread of domestic industries and demographic growth in the seventeenth and eighteenth centuries. The general view seems to be that the 'proto-industrialists' are piling up a new mass of data from regional examples which is impossible to quantify and seems to make any form of generalization almost impossible.[25]

A more positive view can and should be put, however. If localized studies on the development of domestic industries in the period before the advent of industrialization have in many cases made generalization more rather than less difficult, they have greatly widened our understanding of the relatively uncharted geography of European manufacturing and enterprise in a period that was no longer medieval nor yet industrial. They remind us of the extent to which most European societies had already experienced profound and often radical economic and social changes in the preceding centuries, dispelling the notion that industrialization took place in the context of some static and immobile 'traditional' economy. They have reinforced the findings of earlier work on the origins of agricultural specialization not only in England but in many other parts of the Continent, they have shown how previously isolated rural regions were increasingly being drawn into super-regional and even international markets, and on what terms.

More important still, work on 'proto-industrial' communities has generally been concerned to reassert the importance of the social and institutional contexts within which economic growth historically occur-

[25] See D. C. Coleman, 'Proto-industrialization: a concept too many?' *Econ. Hist. Review*, XXXVI (1983), pp. 435–48; Pollard, *Peaceful Conquest and the Industrialization of Europe*, pp. 74–80; O'Brien, 'Do we have a typology', pp. 197–304. For a more positive appraisal see Berg et al., *Manufacture in Town and Country*.

red and with what consequences. As the German historian Ekart Schremmer has put it, if industrialization brought about and indeed necessitated profound changes in social structures and in the organization of production, the converse must also be true. Slow rates of social and institutional change, or even resistance to change, must therefore inhibit economic growth. In that sense, Schremmer has argued, even if proto-industry was not necessarily a step towards industrialization, the study of the role of social institutions in the process of economic change provides an opportunity to invert a 'more narrow and primarily economic approach towards industrialization' focused exclusively on factor flows, factor-price relations, capital formation and shortages, banking and credit systems, entrepreneurial aptitude and so forth. His own comparative studies on southern Germany illustrate well how this can be done in practice, and show, for example, how the spread of rural handicrafts could give rise to a situation of relative self-sufficiency in a rural society composed of small peasant farms in ways that thereafter inhibited the further development of a commercial economy.[26]

Work on proto-industry has not been limited to rural manufacturing alone and others have explored the ways in which work and market-orientated production developed in towns as well as the countryside, in response not only to conventional factors of supply and demand, but also in contexts in which markets and prices were deeply influenced by social institutions.[27] Others have explored the institutional contexts of pre-industrial work, and the influence of social institutions and mentalities on the organization of production. Similar attention to the influence of the essentially non-economic aspects of economic growth is evident in J. K. K. Thomson's recent study of the rise and fall of the Languedoc woollen industry in the seventeenth and eighteenth centuries. Although his subject is not a new 'proto-industry', but rather an old-established staple manufacture producing high quality goods, Thomson shows how the sudden rise and equally sudden fall of the industry in this period owed less to changing market circumstances than to changing forms of organization, in particular mistaken state intervention and slackening entrepreneurial dynamism. Similar factors are also prominent in a recent study of the decline of the Krefeld silk industry in the late eighteenth century by P. Kriedte, who argues that the tendency for an originally new and dynamic elite to become more dependent, more oligarchic and less

---

[26]   E. Schremmer, 'Proto-industrialization: a step towards industrialization?', *J. Europ. Econ. Hist.*, 10:2 (1981), pp. 653–70, esp. 665.

[27]   For example, Berg et al., *Manufacture in Town and Country*.

flexible was a major factor in the decline of the city's principal industry.[28]

If it makes better sense to think of 'proto-industry' as a frame of references rather than a theory, then the important common feature is the emphasis these studies place on the ways in which economic growth has been influenced by social, institutional and other non-economic factors. Although the region or the locality is the preferred focus of 'proto-industrial' studies, they make no attempt to portray the region as an economic unit or to draw a rigid distinction between regional and national economies. Indeed, through the light that is thrown on changing institutional structures and on the impact of administrative and political innovations at a local level, local studies of this sort are often particularly valuable in offering insights into the complex economic and political relationships that existed between the periphery and the centre, the region and the state.

The politics of economic growth

The relations between regional and national economies also raises the question of the role of the state and politics in European industrialization in this period. While economic historians may disagree about many things, there does seem to be a strong consensus in the view that the state played little or no useful part in the development of the early European industrial economies. Professor Pollard puts this argument with particular force, but he is in good company. There are grounds for revising some of these judgements, however.[29]

Even if we are still thinking in terms of regions, it is clear that politics were as important as geography in determining their economic fortunes. It would be impossible not to take account of the critical consequences of the loss of France's colonial economy of the eighteenth century as a result of the Revolution and the Empire, and the resulting decline of an articulated economic system that had focused around the Atlantic seaboard but reached back deep into the interior. As Louis Bergeron and

---

[28]   J. K. K. Thomson, *Clermont-de-Lodève, 1633–1789: Fluctuations in the Prosperity of a Languedocian Cloth-Making Town* (Cambridge, 1982); and 'Variations in industrial structure in pre-industrial Languedoc', in: Berg et al., *Manufacture in Town and Country*, pp. 61–91; P. Kriedte, 'Demographic and economic rhythms: the rise of the silk industry in Krefeld in the 18th century', *J. Europ. Econ. Hist.*, 15:2 (1986), pp. 254–90.

[29]   Pollard, *Peaceful Conquest and the Industrialization of Europe*, pp. 159–63; but cf. Trebilcock, *Industrialization of the Continental Powers*.

others have stressed, not only the geographical axis but indeed the whole character of France's domestic economy was radically and decisively changed as a result.[30]

The same changes impacted on other neighbouring regions as well, making the collapse of the Languedoc woollen industry definitive and deepening the crisis of the Catalan cotton industry that had been provoked by another political event, the loss of Spain's American colonies. The Habsburg Empire, of course, also provides endless examples of the interdependence of politics and regional economics, and it is argued with some energy that the development of the regional economies within the empire cannot be separated from Habsburg imperial politics and preferences which remained primarily political rather than economic in both inspiration and application.[31]

To say that state policies were not always conducive to economic growth is quite different of course from saying that they were of no importance at all. But economics are ultimately inseparable from politics, and politics increasingly adopted well-defined economic objectives. As Louis Bergeron has remarked, for example, the Continental Blockade was 'not just a way of making war, but also a totally new concept of France's economic development, whose base was to be the forceful economic domination of the entire Continent.'

Careful distinctions must be made, however. In what still remains one of the best general essays in English on the role of the state in early industrial development, Professor Barry Supple has argued that the state's contribution to economic growth cannot be seen simply in the narrow terms of mecantilist policies and the attempts to promote particular industries and import substitutes.[32] But even on the narrower front of direct state intervention the argument is by no means closed and recent studies have offered more positive assessments of both the motives and the practical results of French intervention in support of selected industries in the eighteenth century. Thomson's work on the Languedoc woollen industry illustrates how the effects of state intervention were determined very much by time and place – what was beneficial in one decade became constricting in another. In a more recent study of the eighteenth-century Catalan calico printing industry, however, he has also

[30]   Bergeron, *L'Episode Napoléonien*, pp. 208–13.
[31]   N. Gross, 'The Habsburg monarchy, 1750–1914', in: Cipolla (ed.), *The Fontana Economic History of Europe*, vol. 4, 1, pp. 228–78; Ashworth, 'Typologies and evidence'.
[32]   B. Supple, 'The state and the industrial revolution, 1700–1914', in: Cipolla (ed.), *The Fontana Economic History of Europe*, vol. 3, pp. 301–57.

assessed government intervention in a favourable light.[33]

The debates on the ways in which direct and indirect state intervention contributed to industrial development in Germany, Italy and of course Russia do not show any sign of flagging, but it is generally recognized that a broader view is needed of the state's role in promoting institutional as well as economic reform. Most obviously this covers the issue of agrarian reform, the single most important item on the agenda of most European societies in the decades after the emergence of the first industrial economies. Returning for a moment to the comparison between British and European industrialization, it is interesting in this respect that both Crafts and O'Brien single out the relatively small percentage of the agricultural population employed in agriculture in the late eighteenth century as the most distinctive peculiarity of the English economy. Despite the abolition of feudalism in France and Europe after the Revolution, the dead weight of an oversized agrarian population remained one of the most pressing problems for most European countries for the greater part of the nineteenth century – a problem that was all the more difficult to resolve because it was as much (if not more) a problem of internal politics as of economics.

State intervention in the economy also included the whole gamut of institutional and administrative reforms that were the principal legacy of the French Revolution and Napoleonic Empire to the European states. There is already a large corpus of research on some aspects of these changes, particularly on land reform and the consequences of the massive sales of church and crown lands that occurred throughout much of Europe. But about changes in the structure of taxation, the organization of public finances and debts, the impact of legal reform and so forth much less is known. Many economic historians have also drawn attention to the role of 'human capital', in particular literacy and skills, in the process of industrialization, and the provision of those resources cannot be studied without reference to the state and the development of public education.[34]

[33]   P. Deyon and P. Guignet, 'Royal manufactures and the economic progress of France before the industrial revolution', *J. Europ. Econ. Hist.*, 9:3 (1980), pp. 611–32; Thomson, *Clermont de Lodève*; and 'Variations in industrial structure'; but cf. C. Heywood, 'The launching of an "infant industry": the cotton industry of Troyes under protectionism, 1793–1860', *J. Europ. Econ. Hist.*, 10:3 (1981), pp. 553–81, for a less positive assessment.

[34]   Berend and Ranki, *The European Periphery*; and 'Foreign trade and the industrialization of the European periphery'; R. Cameron, 'A new view of European industrialization', *Econ. Hist. Review*, xxxviii:1 (1985), pp. 1–23; L. G. Sandberg, 'Ignorance, poverty and economic backwardness in the early stages of European industrialization. Variations on Alexander Gerschenkron's grand theme', *J. Europ. Econ. Hist.*, 11:3 (1982), pp. 677–82.

Even in the case of more apparently spontaneous processes such as capital formation, the ability or otherwise of the state to provide some element of continuity and some guarantee of public order and political stability cannot be overlooked.

The central issue, as Supple noted, is that 'the state, like the entrepreneur or the labour movement, is a social phenomenon.' However imperfectly, the state represented certain social forces in each society and looked primarily to protect and advance their interests, often at the expense of others. This was why economic change was rarely peaceful, and hence the evolution – as European economic historians have long been aware – of distinctive 'strategies' of development which, given the predominance of the landed classes throughout Continental Europe after 1815, were generally hostile to a process of industrialization along the lines pioneered in the mill towns and factories of Lancashire. Such ideas did not necessarily translate into administrative policies, and even if they did this was no guarantee that they would achieve their ends. As Berend and Ranki rightly emphasize, fear of the consequences of economic growth coexisted with an awareness that economic growth was a necessity for political survival. Such contradictory views could neither absolutely optimize nor inhibit processes of economic development, but they cannot be dismissed as irrelevant either.[35]

To take two neighbouring examples: Italy and Spain. Whether or not unification contributed directly to Italy's economic development, there can be no doubt that Cavour's reform of the Piedmontese state for the first time provided foreign investors with sufficient guarantees to encourage them to make available the capital investment with which northern Italy's new economic infrastructures were created. At the same time, Cavour's strategy was quite deliberately rooted in a vision of an international division of labour in which Italy's future economic prosperity would rest on agriculture. The adoption of free trade looked to integrate Italy into an international economy on the basis of the strength and productivity of its agriculture. Italy's narrow industrial base, which consisted almost exclusively of raw and semi-finished textile production, was quite deliberately subordinated by this strategy. It was only later when free trade was abandoned in favour of protectionism and when the state began for strategic reasons to give indirect and direct subsidies to

[35]   Hostility to industrial values is easily overlooked from an English perspective: see Berend and Ranki, *The European Periphery*: and 'Foreign trade and the industrialization of the European periphery'; Trebilcock, *Industrialization of the Continental Powers*, p. 131; Hardach, 'Some remarks on German economic historiography'.

develop iron and steel making and ship building that the Italian industries began to grow.[36]

A comparison with Spain will not help demonstrate whether Italian government policies were or were not effective in achieving their declared aims, but it can indicate the paramount advantages that followed from the existence of a reasonably secure and autonomous political system. In the Spanish case, the weakness of the state inhibited the formulation of coherent policies and, for example, enabled foreign investors to take control over many of the country's richest natural assets (for example, the Andalusian mercury mines and the Basque ore mines). But the indebtedness of the state itself and the recurrent crises of public finance repeatedly drew capital out of the economy and away from productive investment. Even though Spain's resource endowments were greatly superior to those of Italy, the non-economic constraints on economic growth remained powerful throughout the century.[37]

Conclusion

These references to the importance of the state in the process of European industrialization are not intended as an appeal for a return to an older style of comparative history. It is the great merit of the 'new economic historians' that they have attempted to find ways of moving towards a genuinely comparative study of economic growth, in order to get away from the essentially national boundaries of earlier comparative work. They have also demonstrated the conceptual and empirical errors that derive from approaching European industrialization simply as the emulation of a paradigm of industrialization that was defined through Britain's first industrial revolution. There can be no returning to a single model of industrialization and we have become increasingly aware of the unusual and atypical features of the English case, with respect to the more general European experience of industrialization in the nineteenth century.

The attempts to quantify and measure the key factors and variables in the process of economic growth in Europe in these years have also revealed how few of these are known with any degree of accuracy or certainty. Key indices such as the rate of productivity increase in agriculture remain little more than informed and often highly contradic-

[36]   G. Mori, 'The genesis of Italian industrialization', *J. Europ. Econ. Hist.*, 4:1 (1975), pp. 79–94.
[37]   Nadal, 'Spain 1830–1914'; R. Vaccaro, 'Industrialization in Spain and Italy 1860–1914', *J. Europ. Econ. Hist.*, 1 (1972), pp. 105–19.

tory guesses. Despite the high hopes of the quantifiers it may well be that the element of doubt will remain – but as quantitative analysis becomes more ambitious it has revealed the scale of our uncertainty, and this in turn has added another element of doubt to conventional images and conventional methods.

Having said that, the difficulties, not surprisingly, start as we move from a critique of existing methods to proposals for new methods for the comparative study of European industrialization. The weakness of the alternatives proposed hitherto lies essentially in the fact that they are too often premised on a narrowly economistic understanding of the process of industrialization. Hence the methods advocated are essentially those of historical accounting, which makes it necessary to strip economic history of its social and political contexts. The analysis of economic growth in terms of comparative advantage assumes, for example, an essentially peaceful and harmonious process of expansion and development both internally and internationally. Hence the desire to identify patterns of growth that are claimed to have minimized social tensions. Hence also the widespread belief that state intervention was at best useless and at worst misguided and distorting.

Many will find these arguments unconvincing and will turn to a different view of economic history that is more concerned to locate the processes of industrial development in their specific historical contexts, within the institutions of particular historical societies and within prevailing trends in international relations. Here the methods of historical accounting seem less relevant, since they can seek to comprehend only a relatively small – albeit still important – segment of the broader social and political questions that were as much part and parcel of the European experience of industrialization as spindles and horsepower.

Between these two approaches the divergence is as wide as it has ever been, and shows little sign of diminishing. This explains, in part at least, why the student of European industrialization is confronted by images and interpretations that will seem either contradictory or even worse unrelated to one another. But if there is no easy synthesis within our grasp, we can at least take comfort from the fact that underlying the increasingly technical language and value-free quantitative techniques employed by the historians of European industrialization, there are still fundamentally important issues at stake. The debate on the nature of European industrialization has in fact taken on an exciting new lease of life in recent years. The battle is engaged and we can expect many new contributions and developments in the near future.

4

Financing the Industrial Revolution

Peter Mathias

Absolute shortage of capital has often been put high on the list of those factors which can block or put sharp limits on the rate of economic growth. The general conclusion of contemporaries in the eighteenth century, echoing Adam Smith, was that the principal problems of economic advance lay in the difficulties of 'accumulation' as they termed it – growth in the wealth of nations was principally a function of capital accumulation, with such other relationships as effective demand and technical change being more taken for granted. A few writers, such as Bernard Mandeville, had spoken of the benefits of extravagance and luxury, such spending 'putting the poor on work', but these proponents of conspicuous spending were really arguing against hoarding rather than saving, which was to be the source of accumulation and investment. 'Capitals', wrote Adam Smith roundly, 'are increased by parsimony, and diminished by prodigality and misconduct.' This general stance on the role of accumulation was then taken over from the classical economists by Marx and the Marxist tradition, in parallel to their adaptation of the classical theory of labour value within these assumptions. For them, the primary accumulation of capital, to finance the initial phases of industrialization, of necessity meant depressing consumption standards in the mass market at home to increase investment, or pulling in the surpluses from overseas by exploiting other people.

In the theoretical literature of economic development after 1945 also, the assumption of the problem of absolute shortage of internal savings being the crucial blockage to development was widely accepted. The thesis was often coupled with the complementary notion that pumping in capital would resolve that constraint, implying that managerial efficiency, skills, innovation, an effectively deployed labour force, an adequate market and other factors were dependent variables, which would respond once the capital constraint had been resolved. In consequence of these assumptions much capital was wasted in unrealistic ventures. More recently much greater complexity in these relationships behind growth have been acknowledged; and with this, the status of abundant capital as the principal necessary and sufficient condition, the engine of growth, has declined. Certainly in this simple form the problem of a great scarcity of capital holding back the industrial revolution was a false one for late eighteenth-century England – much more so than for the poorest developing countries of the present day. We may conveniently divide the discussion of capital accumulation and investment in the context of the industrial revolution between an analysis of macro-economic issues and the problem of the micro-economic context of capital investment and credit needs. The first centres on questions of capital supply at the national level and the second on demand at the level of the enterprise.

The national context

The initial assumptions about dramatic short-run increases in the rate of capital formation during the industrial revolution have been virtually reversed. W. W. Rostow assumed that the rate of net capital investment in late eighteenth-century England needed to jump quickly from under 5 per cent of GNP to above 10 per cent, if aggregate annual rates of growth were to rise from under 1 per cent to over 2 per cent, these estimates relying on earlier figures endorsed by W. A. Lewis in relation to contemporary underdeveloped economies. Despite the heroic assumptions required to fill the gaps in data, the actual measurement first attempted by Phyllis Deane suggested quite the opposite process: that the rate of capital investment in Britain rose very slowly from about 5 per cent of national income in the mid-eighteenth century, to about 7 per cent at its end and subsequently reached 10 per cent or a little more only at the end of the 1850s under the great demands of concentrated railway boom years. The later calculations by Professor Feinstein suggest a comparable evolution: rates of total investment (fixed domestic capital formation, increases in stocks and foreign investment) rose from 8 to 14 per cent of gross domestic product between 1770 and 1790–3, which proved to be the maximum percentage (even during the railway age).[1] In turn these

[1]   W. W. Rostow, *The Stages of Economic Growth: A Non-Communist Manifesto* (Cambridge, 1960); W. A. Lewis, *Theory of Economic Growth* (London, 1955); P. Deane 'Capital formation in England before the railway age',

assumptions about the build-up to a higher rate of capital formation over 30 years in the later eighteenth century have been modified by the estimate of N. F. R. Crafts. On the assumption that the economy was growing more slowly, capital investment ratios became more modest – gross domestic investment rising gently from about 5 per cent of GDP in 1750 to about 8 per cent in 1800, to 11.7 per cent in 1831 – a much slower, more gentle path of growth.

Very little support for the thesis that the primary accumulation of capital in the early stages of industrialization perforce depressed living standards, by switching resources from consumption to investment, can be gained from these figures in the debate on the standard of living in the industrial revolution. The standard of living was constrained by other pressures (notably population growth), but scarcely by the scale of the demands of the economy for productive investment. What explains this relatively low level of investment and the slow increase in the investment rate in Britain in these early phases of industrialization? The relatively slow rate of growth of the economy is one principal reason; and this has to be seen in the context of the re-assessment of the rates of growth before 1830 discussed in the initial chapter. Some circularity of argument is possible: one might assert that the low level of investment was itself the cause of the slow rate of growth. But the data on the ability of the economy to mobilize huge resources in wartime suggests that shortage of savings was not itself a prime constraint or a direct cause of slow growth.

Another feature of growth in the eighteenth century was that infrastructure costs were modest, compared with the capital requirements of urbanization and railways in the nineteenth century. Social infrastructure investment in towns and cities lagged (at least in the provision of decent houses for poor working families) and these were great sinks for capital. Much industrial expansion in the eighteenth century, being in rural handicraft industries, did not depend upon such infrastructural investment.

Production technology was also relatively simple and did not make great demands on capital investment (in fixed capital). Much economizing of fixed capital took place, as is discussed below in the section on long-term capital needs. New productive investment paid off in an increasing stream of output in a relatively short time and because of the nature of capital requirements in productive technology the capital:out-

Economic Development and Cultural Change IX (London, 1961); C. Feinstein, 'Capital formation in Great Britain', in: P. Mathias and M. M. Postan (eds), *Cambridge Economic History of Europe*, vol. 7 (Cambridge, 1978), part I, pp. 28–96.

put ratio was quite low. Capital investment in industry, agriculture and transport took place in eighteenth-century Britain under competitive free-market conditions, where profitability was a condition of existence for valorizing the investment. Commercial pressures created incentives to work machines long and hard (subject to technologically imposed limits) and to economize on capital costs as much as possible. No lavish public-sector spending for capital investment occurred in peacetime. The institutional and legal constraints against the public mobilization of capital for corporate enterprise (discussed below), itself forced the need to economize on capital spending and to utilize capital assets as effectively as possible. There may well be a rather different story to tell in very poor economies, facing a twentieth-century scale of technology and social overhead capital in urbanization and transport, aiming to lay down the fixed capitals of a modern economy at ruthless speed by government decree. But this was not the case in eighteenth-century England.

The national framework sets the context. The capital demands for productive investment were slight compared with the savings being poured into other sinks, and compared with the wealth being produced from a resilient, commercially-orientated agriculture, the landed and professional classes, lucrative foreign trade and internal commerce. Consider the single statistic that the total military costs of the French wars for Britain between 1793 and 1815 amounted to approximately £1,000m., with over £500m. in mobilized savings produced for government loans by way of the long-term capital market, spread over 22 years, whereas the total accumulated capital in the canal system, from 1750 to 1820 was about £20m. Moreover, transport investment was one of the 'lumpiest' forms of productive investment to be undertaken. In 1809–10 it was reckoned that annual investment in fixed capital in the entire cotton industry was £0.4m. This was less than 1 per cent of the military budget of £45m. spent during that year. The occasional burst of speculation, exemplified by the South Sea Bubble early in the century, showed how plentiful was the money on offer for 'projects' on such occasions. The financing of canals illustrated the great rise in mobilized savings in provincial towns in England from the mid-century. And these military expenditures for the long French wars between 1793 and 1815 were achieved at a cost of modest inflation (most of the decline in real wages came from higher food prices not directly caused by financing the war), a modest decline in rates of growth, and in the construction industries. Recognizing the other great 'sinks' for the capital of the landed and wealthy classes, no assumption of an aggregate shortage of savings can be entertained.

Some indication of the increase in the general availability of loanable funds (although not necessarily directly in loanable funds to industry and trade) can be gained from the fall in interest rates on government stock – the permanent national debt – where annual rates fell from *c.* 7 per cent in 1700 to 3½ per cent in the 1750s. Mortgage rates followed gilts in this fall, staying between ½ and 1 per cent higher. Between 1714 and 1832 the usury laws imposed a 5 per cent maximum on commercial interest rates.

The context of enterprise

The problems of capital accumulation in the period, therefore, resolve themselves mainly into institutional problems of establishing the means – the legal procedures, the intermediaries, the conduits – whereby existing savings might flow to those in productive enterprise needing credit – to allow thrift to support enterprise. Institutional blockages could exist, traditional motivations could debar these transfers from those receiving most of the savings, even if savings were more than sufficient in aggregate. In part the problem is that of a regional or geographical 'gap' – between the farming savings of East Anglia and the South and South-West and the credit demands of the Midlands and industrializing regions; in part it remained a sociological gap between the entrepreneur in a humble station in life and a landed magnate or prosperous farmer, or a gap in motivation.

The question of conduits, of professional intermediaries, is all the more important given the particular context of eighteenth-century England. There was almost no incorporation allowed for manufacturing industry or limitations of liability for investors in industry – with no appeal possible for public subscriptions for transferable shares, debentures, fixed interest preference shares, or ordinary-share 'risk capital'. The stock exchange, with all its supporting apparatus of brokers and bankers in the capital market, was almost exclusively concerned with government borrowing, growing a very small 'docks and canals' list by the end of the century. The law also prohibited 'sleeping partnerships' in Britain (which played an important role in France) and this meant that no possessors of capital, who did not wish to assume the risks of management and become liable, to the extent of all their private wealth, for the debts of a business, would invest savings in the 'equity' risk capital of a venture. They could make personal loans to businessmen at a fixed rate of interest without incurring this unlimited liability. The government, able to discount commercial risk by drawing on resources through taxation or guaranteeing interest payments on loans, played virtually no part in capital investment in the enterprise sectors of the economy. Moreover, in the early phases of industrialization until towards the end of the eighteenth century, the development of country banking, particularly deposit bank-ing, was very recent and far from complete. Specialized intermediaries and the 'institutions' like bill-brokers and merchant bankers (concerned with internal capital formation), and insurance companies were only beginning to emerge as credit suppliers. The supposed convention of English bankers was not to lend 'long' to industry for fixed investments – and banking capital is the other great source of mobilized institutional savings at this time, apart from Stock Exchange organized capital.

In those special functions in the economy where pre-mobilized capital was demanded in 'lumpy' form – where institutional means of mobilizing investment were essential – legal forms had evolved to accommodate it. Transport investment was effected by canal companies and turnpike trusts, giving the benefits of limited liability for investors, the advantages of incorporation for the operators, and legal powers to overcome incalcitrant minorities through, for example, compulsory purchase of land. Public utility investment also embraced warehouse and dock companies. Trustees established under private equitable trusts were enabled to raise capital for many purposes of 'social overhead' invest-ment, such as docks. The ownership of ships was broken down into very small fractions – down to 'sixty-fourths' or smaller, which became transferable pieces of property for investment. Similar legal devices such as 'cost-book' arrangements made the capital for Cornish mines equally divisible and some mines could operate as companies with transferable shares. Risks could be spread by all these means. An efficient mortgage market existed to help investment in land improvements, enclosure acts and drainage acts. Insurance companies, where very large capitals needed to be associated with risk spreading, requiring a wide capital base, were also accommodated by the parliamentary process, but the individual insurance underwriter, with informal syndicates, had already become characteristic of the English insurance market in shipping. Judging by interest rates, capital was plentiful in those normal years unaffected by monetary crises or large government borrowing, fluctuating from 3–5 per cent in the gilt-edged market and 4–5 per cent in the mortgage market, throughout the period of the industrial revolution, save only during some years in wartime (particularly during the Napoleonic Wars).

Where large capitals had to be mobilized in advance, and where capital charges (the annual interest payments on capital borrowed) formed a high proportion of the total annual costs of a venture – in the construction industries and public utility investment fields above all – then low interest rates did encourage enterprise. Booms clustered in times of cheap credit; and faded when interest rates got pushed up and the flow of loanable funds became diverted into more profitable channels, particularly by the

5 per cent usury law 'cut-off'. These sorts of investment were much involved in institutional ways of mobilizing capital for investment. The debate about the importance of the rate of interest in capital accumulation for long ignored the nature of the investment in question. It has until now been conducted almost without a mention of the context of price movements. Higher interest rates, if the capital is available for borrowing, will be less of a deterrent in a time of inflation; because postponing the investment until interest rates fall may incur higher costs, from the rise in prices, than would be incurred by the higher interest charges. One has to discount the rate of inflation from the rate of interest, by deducting the annual percentage rise in prices from the annual cost of borrowing to arrive at the 'real' rate of interest, and conversely with falling prices. Inflation benefits the borrower at fixed rates, at the same time as it prejudices the lender; and deflation in the opposite way. This clearly explains in large measure the great increase in enclosure (and banks lending to agriculture) during the Napoleonic Wars, when interest rates were high but agricultural prices were also rising.

The importance of lower rates of interest, however, is not so clearly apparent with manufacturing industry, at least in long-term borrowing, and personal lending. Most personal lending and long-term loans tended to run at 5 per cent – borrowed in pounds repaid in guineas. Small differences in the cost of credit was not as significant a variable to an entrepreneur in manufacturing industry as to a builder or the financial backer of a building, because the difference did not create such a difference in his total costs – he turned his capital over much faster. The known availability of credit, not small variations in its price, was the key here. Samuel Gurney, the bill broker, spoke also for merchants and industrialists in the eighteenth century when he appeared as a witness before a parliamentary committee in 1833. 'I think it is very important to the commercial interest', he replied to questions about the economic effects of high interest rates, 'that the facilities in procuring discounts should be great, but not of great importance what the rate of interest is . . . whether he pays two and a half, three or three and a half [per cent], is not of much importance. It is of much less importance in comparison with having unlimited facility in procuring discounts.'[2] In later times, and today, bank-rate policy varying interest rates has affected the level of activity and investment in building much more than in manufacturing industry.

[2]   Parl. Papers Committee on Manufactures, Commerce and Shipping (1833), QQ 150–1. He did admit that interest rates of 5% or 10% would impose a burden.

Capital structure and short-term credit

The capital structure of eighteenth-century manufacturing industry is also relevant in considering the nature and problems of capital accumulation: obviously the structure of assets conditions the nature of the credit sought and the means by which it can be provided. In the pre-factory domestic system, almost all capital was embodied in stocks (in raw-material stocks, goods 'in the pipe-line' during manufacture, goods in process of being sold); virtually none in specialized fixed capital at all. Almost all costs, therefore, were variable costs – materials and labour; not overhead costs – capital charges, maintenance, depreciation. The assets of a large weaving concern at the end of the century were over £180,000, with total plant valued at just over £160 – simply the warehouse – and stock at over £120,000, and normal commercial debtors almost £60,000.[3] Even the most heavily capitalized of large-plant industrial concerns in the late eighteenth century had relatively small percentages of their total assets in fixed capital – buildings and machinery: iron works up to 50 per cent; a typical large London brewery 10 to 15 per cent. The spinning and printing firms quoted by Dr Edwards range from under 1 per cent (quite atypical for a mill), to 15, 17, and 20–35 per cent. Mines would be different. A very highly capitalized large-scale London brewery provides an example. Truman, Hanbury and Buxton's accounts for 1800 show total gross assets to have been £334,000 – a vast manufacturing plant for its time. Of this total beer stocks were £100,000, raw material stocks £75,000, trade debts (i.e. beer delivered but not yet paid for, together with loans) £100,000. 'Fixed stock', public-house leases and casks together totalled only £50,000, of which the actual brewery and its plant, excluding casks, came to only £26,000. This was typical for a large-scale manufacturing business in general by reason of the *extent* of the fixed capitals employed.[4]

The importance of such an asset structure is at once apparent when the sources of credit for eighteenth-century industry are analysed. Short-

---

[3] M. M. Edwards, *Growth of the British Cotton Trade, 1780–1815* (Manchester, 1967), p. 257, table E/1.

[4] The proportion which fixed assets bore to total assets, or to turnover, depended greatly upon whether buildings and machines were rented, not owned. A highly 'geared' business, in this sense, would have a lower proportion of fixed capital than a business which owned all its buildings and plant. In this case the value of the site did not feature in the totals – and this was usually the case in eighteenth-century accounts. The buildings, plant and stock were effectively valued, on the other hand, for insurance purposes.

term credit requirements were by far the greatest need quantitatively to finance raw-material purchases, stocks, and discounting bills of exchange arising from sales to get back into cash before the customary credit period was up. The traditional 3–6 month credit period in raw-material purchasing in cotton, for example, often allowed spinners to get cash for their sales of yarn (by discounting the bills of exchange) before they had to put down cash for the raw cotton purchases that went into these sales. Dealers and yarn merchants could often give credit, or short-term accommodation, to allow manufacturers a cushion of credit on the selling side of the business. The short-term lending on overdrafts and the discounting activity of banks propped up this sort of credit flow to the manufacturers direct, or to the manufacturers via the merchants. The dominance of bills of exchange in Lancashire as a circulating medium, the dominant mode of settling commercial transactions by the bill on London, short-term credit in discounting, the short-term bank overdraft or loan as the crucial credit requirement of industry, all fitted into this asset structure.

Even if the generalization is correct that British banks only lent short – and there is more to be said about that[5] – this still meant that the banks were financing by far the largest credit needs of business, given such an asset structure. By the end of the century, too, inter-regional flows of short-term credit were beginning to be significant between country banks in different parts of the country, particularly in the discount market for bills of exchange. At the end of the century this rising traffic in bills had induced into existence a new sort of financial intermediary – the bill broker or discount house. When a function becomes 'institutionalized' with the appearance of new specialist intermediaries, it is a principal sign of a widening market, and mounting transactions. Such professional intermediaries existed on an increasing scale in eighteenth-century England, principally serving an informal local capital market – whether scriveners, bankers, local attorneys, land agents – as well as London-based insurance companies or bill brokers. Through them flows of credit, lending and borrowings were much easier than in a face-to-face situation involving direct transfers and confrontations, when both the geographical and the sociological gaps proved harder to span.

Long-term capital needs and responses

Long-term capital could still be a crucial problem though. Where did it

[5]   See below, pp. 82–4.

come from? Often it is unrealistic in eighteenth-century terms to put a firm line between long-term capital and short-term credit. The greatest source was undoubtedly 'plough-back', particularly for the established firm already over the 'hump' of initial investments in 'lumpy' plant. It is still by far the largest source of industrial investment in the twentieth century. As T. S. Ashton concluded: 'The records of firm after firm tell the same story . . . the proprietors agree to pay themselves small salaries, restrict their household expenses and put their profits to reserve.'[6] 'Plough-back' is in some ways the wrong concept: the profits were never taken out of the business in the first place. Although aggregate rates of investment did not rise dramatically, enclaves of very high investment (as in the cotton industry) at particular times and in individual firms demanded such a social response, given the dominance of the family firm, which remained characteristic of the ownership of industry. But the heroic days were soon over. Once well established, in normal years (but not in abnormal years) one might presume that the demands of the business did not preclude social expenditure in keeping with the status brought by wealth – which usually meant acquiring a landed estate to some degree.

But this is far from being the end of the story. There has to be some capital in the first place to establish the business. At certain times entrepreneurs might wish, or be compelled, to invest capital for expansion at a faster rate than profits were accumulating. Any expansion might require a piece of 'lumpy' investment, involving borrowing and subsequent repayment over a term of years. In a time of business depression, in a liquidity crisis, the business could need hard cash urgently to pay creditors who were unwilling to 'fund' their claims on the firm any longer, or to satisfy the most pressing cash need of all, wages. Although not typical, these times might be crucial for an enterprise – for its foundation, its expansion or its survival.

How did industrialists respond to such circumstances, remembering the virtual prohibition of incorporation and limitation of liability for suppliers of risk capital? In the first place the initial size of capitals was remarkably small, even in many large-plant industries like iron or cotton-spinning. Capital-saving techniques were widely used: renting premises, even machines or power; converting existing buildings cheaply; not building grandly from scratch in the first place; above all, beginning in a small way in fixed capital and being much dependent on credit from one's suppliers or customers. Merchant suppliers could be much more important than is usually suggested. One of the remarkable things about

[6]   T. S. Ashton, *The Industrial Revolution, 1760–1830* (London, 1968).

industrial change in eighteenth-century England is just how extensive were these 'capital-economizing' techniques employed, particularly those designed to conserve cash outlays and investment in fixed capital. In the initial phases of developing new technology which required new machinery or power, old buildings were adapted in very makeshift fashion, corn mills modified for other purposes, buildings leased and rented rather than bought outright. Machinery was simple, run up on the spot very often by a carpenter and blacksmith with a clockmaker; mill buildings were filled with machines only gradually. One could 'get off the ground', that is to say, in industries only just beginning to adopt the technology of massive production, with very modest capital outlays in the first years. And raw materials could be gained on credit from merchants, with any luck.

When the business was established, successful and yielding profits, then the characteristic decision would be taken to build the splendid new mill. The present-day industrial archaeologist's delight was almost certainly not the initial premises of a new firm. If an entrepreneur, his family, his wife and her family, had any freehold land or property – however modest – then raising a mortgage could be a key instrument for getting a loan. Freehold land was the best security available in eighteenth-century England and the mortgage market was perhaps the most traditional means of raising cash, the most well-tried, trusted and cheap. Apart from possible negotiations for larger transactions in London, flourishing local long-term lending existed in the mortgage market and the local attorney or land agent was often the key figure or the key intermediary. A lot of money passed through his hands in trust funds or on deposit which could be safely invested on such security. In the cotton areas an active market in property clearly flourished, with owners offering to rent, or convert and rent, premises to spinners and printers, as an independent commercial activity in the property market. Landowners and petty property owners made an indirect contribution to the provision of industrial capital in this way, as they did by investing in canals or mines.

Where relatively small capitals were involved – as they so often were with newer entrants to even the largest-plant industries and to most entrepreneurs in small-plant or domestic industry – and depending on the family group, kinship contacts and other personal acquaintances were usually the first to be exploited. Late eighteenth-century business operated in a predominantly face-to-face world of friends, cousins, business associates. This world was the first recourse for cash beyond the web of credit that all firms were supported by in their day-to-day transactions. The resources which could be drawn in through this network were limited in scale, except for businessmen lucky enough to find themselves members of very wealthy and extensive kinship groups – such as the

Quaker dynasties. But the initial requirements were, very often, astonishingly small and in conjunction with capital-economizing devices very many of the short-term credit arrangements could be 'funded' to extend loans for a larger span – at 5 per cent p.a. In addition, even though without benefit of limitation of liability, people with some capital but no desire to manage did offer themselves as partners – in fact 'sleeping', in law 'managing' – despite the hazards this presented to their personal fortunes if the business fell into debt. Not uncommonly a young person, such as Robert Owen, or Samuel Whitbread, coming into an industry without family ownership or much capital behind him, needed to take a partner in order to get launched independently in the trade. In the spectrum of partnership functions lying between supplying finance and management usually the young man of vigour began with very little (but some) capital and supplied most of the management expertise, while the older partner contributed mainly capital (and held a watching brief to secure his holding). As the managing partner built up his holding there came the point, at the end of a fixed term of the partnership (as such partnerships traditionally were) where he would go it alone; once he had the capital he wanted to be boss in his own firm. Where immense capitals were needed, or where risks were very high – as in banking or London brewing in the late eighteenth century – then more than one principal was usually advantageous, if not inevitable.

An analysis of capital investment shows extreme diversity in the sources of capital – a surprising range in the 'length' of lending – so the main conclusion must be that, despite formal limitations in the main institutional means of mobilizing capital, the context had remarkable flexibility and resilience, both from within the commercial spectrum enfolding industry and from the general social context facing entrepreneurs; and that the initial capital requirements for entrants were astonishingly small. Very modest savings (or access to modest savings) plus a good local credit rating, plus being of accepted standing in local society and in the trade were the crucial requisites, even if at quite a humble level. The great emphasis given to personal probity, honesty of dealing and a good reputation in the homilies written about business success relate exactly to the need to acquire credit in this context of business. Two instances from contemporary diaries illustrate the financial barriers to entry and the ways in which they were overcome – in a world of face-to-face contacts, kinship groups, close friends and associates in business, where personal probity and trust were of the essence in gaining credit. And credit, with the longer-term borrowing which might develop from short-term credit, was of the essence in getting started. The first instance concerns a new entrant to cotton spinning in 1817, when David

Whitehead and his brothers were seeking to set up their own cotton business. The business of

> Warbourton, who had the mill of whom we took [i.e. rented] the room . . . was not doing well for him. He said if we had no objections he would deliver up the mill to us. We went with him to Mr. Hargreaves, of whom he rented the mill, but did not agree . . . at that time. We found that with all the money we could collect together we had little enough. We got mother to go and see if she could prevail of old Mr. Thomas Hoyle of Manchester (Printer) to lend us a hundred pounds. My grandfather Lionel Blakey was one of the 'friends' (called Quakers), as was also Thomas Hoyle. They were relations and fellow play[mates] as boys.[7]

An even more graphic description reveals William Stout's beginnings as a shopkeeper in Lancaster in 1687:

> So soone as I had taken a shop, I applyed to my mother and brother in order to get what money I could of what was due by my father's will, which was fifty pound let by my father upon bond to John Hodgson, merchant, designed for me, and 3*l*. 10*s*. intrest. And I sould 3 acres of land in Kelet Intacks to Henry Batson for 33*l*.; and some land my father bought of George Gardner I sould to my brother Josias for 33*l*.; left me by my father's will, in all, 119*l*. 10*s*. and I borrowed twelve pound which I repayed the 2nd of 12 mo: following, so that the said 119*l*. 10*s*. was all that I could command as due by my father's will. And I borrowed of my sister 10*l*. which I kept many years. . . . And my brother Josias ofring to lend me a horse, I made ready for the jurney and tooke with me 120*l*. of the aforesaid summe. . . . And we all got well to London in five days, and lodged at the Swan with Two Necks in Lad Laine. And as soone as I got there I applyed to such tradesmen as I was recomended to, and bought of sundry persons goods to the value of two hundred pounds or upwards, and payed each of them about halfe ready money, as was then usual to do by any young man beginning trade.[8]

A different instance from the opposite end of the spectrum of scale and capitalization in eighteenth-century business is offered by the diary of Mrs Thrale, describing how her husband's large porter brewery, one of the largest industrial plants in the kingdom, got through the depression and monetary crisis in 1772, when they were short of cash even to pay wages:

[7]   H. I. Hunt, *David Whitehead of Rawtenstall*, quoted in M. W. Flinn (ed.), *Readings in Economic and Social History* (London, 1964), pp. 96–9.
[8]   J. D. Marshall, *The Autobiography of William Stout of Lancaster, 1665–1752* (Manchester, 1967), p. 89.

First we made free with our mother's money ... about 3000£ 'twas all she had; and big as I was with child I drove down to Brighthelmstone to beg of Mr. Scrase ... 6,000£; dear Mr. Scrase was an old gouty solicitor, friend and contemporary of my husband's father. Lady Lade [Thrale's sister] lent us 5000£ more.

Mrs Thrale prepared to mortgage all her own estates in N. Wales and to cut the timber on them – usually a landowner's first line of financial reserves because timber was virtually cash in standing form. But the main creditors in the end – perforce – were the malt and hop merchants, who supplied long-term credit by default rather than by design. Their bills of £130,000 (the main outgoings of the business, apart from wage payments) just remained unpaid for some years, the balances earning 5 per cent p.a.

The role of the banks

It is appropriate here to consider the role of the banks in capital formation, even though their institutional development has not been discussed. The main role of the banks, which has been stressed already, was that they lent 'short' and also through their note issues created currency – circulating media – at the same time, by providing their own notes for overdrafts, short-term loans, and discounting bills of exchange. They were not only intermediaries between borrowers and lenders but creators of credit themselves. Bankers were also involved in longer-term lending more than the older books on banking history acknowledged. This was not a permanent or regular structural feature of capital formation in Britain during the industrial revolution (as it became, for example, in Germany in the later nineteenth century), but nevertheless it could still be crucial at certain times of expansion or survival for a business (though not so much for it becoming established in the first place). As the business histories accumulate so the generalizations need adjusting.

Most of the famous names in industry were associated at certain times with bank lending. Some formed alliances with bankers or became bankers themselves when wealthy – Strutt, Arkwright, Oldknow, most of the large London brewers (and many brewers in provincial towns), Cornish mine adventurers, Kentish papermakers. The Carron Iron Works was indebted for many years to Scottish and London bankers; Boulton borrowed from the Hopes of Amsterdam; the Duke of Bridgewater owed £25,000 to his bankers while the canal project was stretching his family resources. The present list of over fifty instances will certainly lengthen and this is only of known, *direct* lending. The same is true of the link between bankers and transport investment, through their becoming treasurers of turnpike trusts and canal companies. Often bankers found themselves of necessity supplying credit to the venture. At one stage removed, the nexus between banker and long-term lending was still wider, even if very much more difficult to identify in the ledgers of bank or business, when the banker was propping up a merchant or a landowner or a professional man who was, in turn, a long-term creditor in a manufacturing business or a mine.

Sometimes such long-term financing happened by default rather than by design (as with mercantile creditors). A banker lent short for three months or six months, and then found that he could not get his money back at the due date. Provided the business was essentially sound and suffering only a liquidity crisis that time would cure (and even sometimes if it was not), the banker's interests were usually best served by not foreclosing – not putting the debtor in Chancery and the assets of the firm under the hammer. The fixed assets of a manufacturing concern do not at all represent its true value, which is a function of the earning power of the business. Buyers at a forced auction might well be reticent about such specialized assets, so the sale of the buildings and plant would probably realize only a few shillings in the pound. Only the lawyers would benefit, particularly with the complexities, delays and high costs of legal processes in the late eighteenth century. The larger the loan the more the banker's own fate was bound up with the survival of the business which had borrowed it. There are said to be two ways of receiving solicitous attention from a banker: either having a very large sum of your money on deposit with him; or being in the possession of a very large loan of his money. For these reasons it was usually much better for a large creditor to hang on at 5 per cent p.a., particularly if the loan tied the debtor's custom for commercial or financial dealings with his creditor – which might be conducted with less keen prices in such circumstances.

Even without such constraints short-term loans – the outstanding 'float' of credit, on overdraft, even if it was turned over regularly – might well become an instrument of long-term finance simply for the mutual convenience of both parties. The banker felt secure in that permission had to be sought for renewal every few months, but the industrialist felt he had great flexibility with the assumption that in normal times he might anticipate renewal. The credit links were often more intimate than the business records of either banks or firms reveal. Bankers became wealthy men who sometimes put their profits, withdrawn from the bank as their personal estate, into other businesses as partners or as personal creditors, even where they did not put their customers' deposits at risk in his way. These credits would not appear on the books of the bank, having been withdrawn as profits. More generally, the instability of English banking in the first century of industrialization, when country banks collapsed in scores in every major monetary crisis, suggests that their portfolios were very much more long-term in fact than they admitted to parliamentary committees or advised that they should be in principle. Mining banks in Cornwall, hop merchant banks in Southwark were notoriously unstable. In the collapse of agricultural prices after 1815 many country banks were brought down. All this suggests that the fortunes of the banks were committed to lending long, by default or by design, more than has been supposed. Indeed, one strongly suspects that historians may have been deceived by what the leaders of the banking profession told public enquiries about the traditional rules of their mystery, and by what eminent bankers (often the most well established and conservative) wrote about the 'principles' of English banking – of how it *ought* to be conducted – into believing that this was itself the norm for all English bankers in practice. There may well also have been a false sense of perspective in time, contributing to this underestimate of the role of the banks in capital formation. After 1850, with the consolidation of English banking with large, multi-branch, nation-wide businesses, conservatism and a 'safe' lending policy were generalized, with strict limitations in the freedom of action of local branch managers imposed by head office. But to read this norm into country banking at the end of the eighteenth century is unreal. Indeed, the instability of English banking (in contrast to, say, the Scottish or the French) suggests an almost opposite conclusion – that 'expansionist' credit practices increased the dimensions of industrial and commercial expansion as much as they heightened fluctuations by intensifying monetary crises. As R. E. Cameron concludes: 'In the final analysis the remarkable feature of the intermixture of banking and industry is not that so many banks came to grief as a result, but that so many vigorous and progressive industries developed from it.'[9]

But the main issue, in the last analysis, is that the bulk of credit required by a business in trade and manufacturing industry in the eighteenth century was trade credit and short-term loans supplying the needs of circulating capital. And by supplying these needs, by lending on security or 'by note of hand', by discounting bills, or by overdrafts operating through cheque accounts, the banks were performing the key credit function, and thereby releasing the internal resources of firms, and such capital as they could collect from other sources, for long-term investment. In this way the English banking system contributed to the

[9]   R. E. Cameron, *Banking in the Early Stages of Industrialisation* (Oxford, 1967), p. 58.

expansionary forces, because the country bank was not at this time 'primarily a broker between lenders (depositors) and borrowers' but an 'engine of credit', however puny, pumping out a stream of new money by issuing currency, or creating deposits, bank money, by overdraft with drafts and cheques.[10]

Recent studies (not cited in footnotes)

General

R. E. Cameron, 'A new view of European industrialisation', *Economic History Review* XXXVIII (1985); N. F. R. Crafts, 'Patterns of development in nineteenth-century Europe', *Oxford Economic Papers* XXXVI (1984); F. Crouzet, *De la Supériorité de l'Angleterre* . . . (Paris, 1985); P. Deane, *The First Industrial Revolution* (Cambridge, 1979); J. R. Hicks, *A Theory of Economic History* (Oxford, 1969); E. L. Jones, *The European Miracle* (Cambridge, 1981); D. Landes, *The Unbound Prometheus* (Cambridge, 1965); Peter Mathias, *The First Industrial Nation* (London, 1983); *The Transformation of England* (London, 1979); E. A. Wrigley, *Continuity, Chance and Change* (London, 1989).

Particular themes

M. Berg, P. Hudson and M. Sonenschem, *Manufactures in Town and Country before the Factory* (Cambridge, 1983); D. C. Coleman, 'Proto-industrialisation: a concept too many?', *Economic History Review* XXXVI (1983); P. Kriedte, H. Medick and J. Schlumbohm, *Industrialisation before Industrialisation* (Cambridge, 1981); P. H. Lindert and J. G. Williamson, 'Re-interpreting Britain's social tables, 1688–1913', *Explorations in Economic History* XX (1983) – see also *Idem.* XIX (1982); R. Samuel, 'The workshop of the world . . .' *History Workshop* III (1977); J. G. Williamson, *Did British Capitalism Breed Inequality?* (London, 1985); E. A. Wrigley and R. S. Schofield, *The Population History of England, 1541–1871* . . . (London, 1981).

[10]   Ibid.

5

Transport: the Survival of the Old beside the New

T. C. Barker

During the industrial revolution, which we shall interpret generously as stretching from the mid-eighteenth century to the mid-nineteenth, so as to take in the early Railway Age, greater output was obtained in transport, as in manufacturing industry, by applying a rapidly increasing labour force (resulting from considerable population growth) to existing, but often better organized, methods of production, as well as by using new mechanical techniques and applying power-driven machinery. The latter, of course, provided the real spearhead of change and made possible quantum leaps in labour productivity; but the contribution of the former, overwhelmingly predominant at the beginning of the period and of considerable significance at its conclusion, ought not to be underestimated and certainly not overlooked.

Transport historians, who used to concentrate on the new – often because it was better documented – are now beginning to pay more attention to the survival, and the spread, of the old. They no longer dwell so much on canals and railways but realize that coastal and river traffic continued to be of growing importance and that horse-drawn road transport was increasingly used, until mechanical traction began to replace it over half a century *after* railways began to appear on the British scene. At sea, although steam vessels began to be used commercially for short river journeys, coastal trips or sea crossings from the end of the Napoleonic wars, inefficient low-pressure engines demanded so much fuel per mile travelled that many years were to elapse – until the later nineteenth century in fact – before steam eclipsed sail on longer voyages.[1]

[1] G. S. Graham, 'The ascendancy of the sailing ship, 1850–85', *Economic History Review*, IX (1956), pp. 74–88.

Photographs of Cape Town harbour taken during the Boer War reveal a forest of masts.

It is important at the outset to realize that there are two basically different sorts of traffic, each of which calls for a different mode of transport. Category one comprises heavy, bulky goods of low value, such as coal, grain or stone, where the transport cost element in relation to the total cost is high. Category two is made up of high value goods such as gems at one extreme, but also including costly imports, spices for instance, or on a far greater scale the whole range of manufactures to which value has been added. In the first category low transport costs per ton carried, not speed, are of primary importance. In the second, speed in getting goods to market (and being paid for them) is paramount. The carriage of passengers and mails also comes into this second category. Water transport, capable of carrying 20–30 tons on an inland waterway or up to 300–400 tons in a coastal vessel, was the bulk carrier; horse-drawn road transport provided greater speed, especially when roads were improved and services better organized.

Britain as a whole, and England in particular, was blessed by nature with much naturally navigable water. Because it was a narrow island, coastal shipping was able to serve many places, not only on the coast itself but also for considerable distances inland up river estuaries. London, the country's main port, lay more than 40 miles from the open sea as the crow flies and even further if measured along the river Thames itself downstream from London Bridge, the limit of navigation for seagoing vessels. From the Wash, farther north on the east coast, several rivers provided water communication as far inland as Peterborough, Bedford and Cambridge. Further north still, the Trent, a tributary of the Humber, put Nottingham, far inland, into direct communication with the sea and the Ouse performed the same function for York. On the other side of the country, that vast estuary the Bristol Channel served Bristol and Cardiff directly, and from it the Severn penetrated deep inland as far as Shrewsbury, while its tributary, the Avon, allowed vessels to reach Stratford. Professor Wilson has shown how, from the beginning of the seventeenth century onwards, river improvement, involving the building of locks and weirs as well as the cutting off of awkward meanders, enlarged this waterway network either by extending navigation farther upstream, or by bringing other rivers into the system, or by enabling larger vessels to navigate stretches already navigable for smaller ones. In three much-copied maps he has revealed at a glance how much more of the country was brought within 15 miles of navigable water before the coming of modern canals in the middle of the eighteenth century.[2] That they were late arrivals was not a sign of British backwardness. The country was already well served with waterways for the carriage of heavy, bulky goods long before that.

More attention is now being paid to London's remarkable growth during the sixteenth and seventeenth centuries (its population increased from 40,000 to close on 600,000 in that time) in explaining Britain's early take-off into self-sustained growth.[3] Most of the grain supply needed to keep alive this huge, growing metropolitan population had to come by water, most of it from farms in communication with the Thames, for it was bulky and of low value. As demand grew, so supplies had to be brought down the coast from farther afield. Without extensive water communication, many years before the age of canals, London's growth would have been arrested. The capital's essential fuel, coal, also depended on water transport. Professor Flinn, in his volume dealing with the British coal industry between 1700 and 1830, has shown that at the beginning of that period London was consuming about 15 per cent of Britain's entire coal output. Supplies came coastwise from the north-east, especially from the Tyne which, he estimates, was responsible for over 40 per cent of the country's entire coal output.[4] By then the north-east coalfield had already attracted to it various furnace industries, notably glassmaking and salt boiling, the products of which also depended almost entirely upon coastal shipping for their distribution.

As the traffic in bulky goods of low value grew during the eighteenth century, so existing arrangements were further extended. River improvement continued (water communication was obtained from Liverpool to Manchester, for instance, by the opening of the Mersey–Irwell navigation from Warrington to Manchester by 1740) and more vessels were employed in the coastal trade. Canals began to be built only when access was required to part of the country where there was no improvable river.

This occurred first of all in the mid-eighteenth century in south-west Lancashire, where the Liverpool merchants wished to gain access by water to the coalfield, at and about what subsequently came to be known as St Helens. There was a thriving salt trade through Liverpool, which

[2]   T. S. Wilson, *River Navigation in England, 1600–1750* (Oxford, 1936; repr. 1964). See also the same writer's *The Coasting Trade, 1600–1750* (Manchester 1938; repr. 1967).
[3]   F. J. Fisher, 'London as an "engine of economic growth"' in: J. S. Bromley and E. H. Kossman, *Britain and the Netherlands in Europe and Asia* (London, 1968).
[4]   M. W. Flinn, *The History of the British Coal Industry*, vol. 2, *The Industrial Revolution* (Oxford, 1984), pp. 26, 274.

Liverpool had already encouraged in 1732 by making the river Weaver navigable from Frodsham Bridge up to the saltfield. Much of the coal required to boil this salt had to be carried overland from the south-west Lancashire coalfield to the Mersey, adding greatly to its cost, and thence up the Weaver or to the rock salt works on the Mersey itself. Other supplies required for domestic or industrial purposes in the city, had also to be carried expensively overland. Liverpool Corporation, representing the merchants there, obtained parliamentary sanction in 1755 to build a waterway from the coalfield to the Mersey. The Sankey Canal was carrying traffic by November 1757. Coal costing 4s. 2d. per 'long' ton of 30 cwt (the local measure) at the colliery was sold to Liverpool householders for 7s. 6d. at a time when the overland journey of ten miles would have doubled or trebled the pithead price.[5]

So began Britain's Canal Age. The Sankey Canal was followed soon afterwards by the better-known waterway from Worsley to Manchester, built for the Duke of Bridgewater. It was opened for part of the way in 1761 and throughout by the middle of 1765. It had a similar cost-reducing effect on the transport, and therefore the retail price, of goods. These pioneer ventures encouraged a spate of canal building during the 1760s and 1770s. There was then a period of quiescence, followed by an even greater enthusiasm for canals, the so-called 'canal mania', in the 1790s. Meanwhile the existing river and coastal traffic, using larger vessels, continued to grow and flourish. Canal transport supplemented it, though it was of great importance for areas, like that round St Helens, untraversed by navigable river. A whole region, Birmingham and the Black Country, came into this category and was particularly indebted to the new deadwater navigations. Canals were also of significance in providing competition for the river navigations. They did not carry all, nor indeed perhaps even the greater part, of inland and coastal waterborne traffic. It was not until the beginning of the nineteenth century, over 40 years after the Canal Age began, that a direct canal link was made between the Midlands and London. Until then existing water communication via the river Trent or, later, via the river Thames from Oxford, had sufficed.[6]

Canals, of course, were of importance from the point of view of company promotion and the raising of capital from the public at large by means of joint stock companies. The Acts of Parliament which gave them joint stock status foreshadowed those for railways. But the capitals

---

[5]   T. C. Barker, 'The beginnings of the Canal Age in the British Isles', in: L. S. Pressnell (ed.), *Studies in the Industrial Revolution* (London, 1960).

[6]   For which see J. R. Ward, *The Finance of Canal Building in Eighteenth-Century England* (Oxford, 1974).

involved were relatively small: the Sankey was built for under £20,000 and many of the others for under £100,000. Only one or two of the later canals of the 'mania' period exceeded £1,000,000.[7] Nor did these canals, many of them built for narrow boats, demand large amounts of building material. The engineering involved was already familiar to river improvers, though water supply did pose new problems. There was nevertheless a substitution of fixed for working capital, a lowering of transport costs and, above all, a prevention of bottlenecks developing in the carriage of coal and other bulky, low-cost items. We do need, however, to see water transport as a whole: the continued development of the old as well as the spread of the new.

We must now consider the second category of traffic: the carriage by road over medium and long distances, of passengers and lighter goods of greater value such as the mails, imported goods and manufactures of various sorts to which value had been added. The older writers used to belittle improvements in road transport before the early nineteenth century and the work of men like McAdam and Telford. They drew attention to Arthur Young's adverse comments on certain stretches of road which he traversed between 1768 and 1770, as he toured various parts of the country.[8] Sidney and Beatrice Webb, in their volume on the 'King's Highway', published in 1913, confirmed this view. In their apparently careful piece of research they poured scorn on the inefficiency of local statute labour and the incompetence of local farmers who took turns as highway surveyors. The turnpiking of the eighteenth century, they went on to argue, did not improve matters, for all this activity was piecemeal:

> If, during the eighteenth century, anyone had taken the trouble to make a turnpike map of England, this would have shown, not a system of radiating arteries of communication, but scattered cases of turnpike administration, unconnected with each other ... It took, in fact, practically a whole century of disconnected effort before even such national arteries of communication as the Great North Road from London to Edinburgh, the Irish road from London to Holyhead, or the great western road from London to Exeter came, for the whole of their lengths, under the administration of Turnpike Trusts ...[9]

[7]   Ibid., ch. 2.
[8]   For examples, see G. E. Mingay (ed.), *Arthur Young and His Times* (London, 1975), pp. 154–8.
[9]   S. and B. Webb, *The Story of the King's Highway* (London, 1913), p. 125.

Taking her cue from them, Lilian Knowles, the first professor of economic history at London University, told her readers in 1921:

> The public highways of Great Britain had been until the eighteenth century mere earthen tracks or bridle paths for pack mules and riders ... Wheeled traffic, though beginning, was still uncommon at the end of the seventeenth century ... These wheeled vehicles increasing in numbers wore the earthen surface of the highways into great ruts and the roads became more of a scandal at a time when it became more and more necessary to be able to move masses of raw material or manufactured goods ...[10]

Even so late as 1965, Professor Charles Wilson, in his very useful textbook covering 1603–1763, concluded that in those years English roads 'were everywhere deplorable and getting steadily worse'.[11]

We now see the true position very differently. The Southampton brokage books, which recorded tolls paid by carts leaving that port town so early as 1443/4, reveal a remarkable volume of cart traffic, some of it bound for destinations quite far away: for instance, 50 journeys to Coventry (130 miles) and 54 to Oxford, and in fact in all directions apart from the south-west, where the tracks remained impassable for wheeled vehicles. London (80 miles) received 535 carts that year in preference to what we might guess would be the more attractive alternative, coastal vessels. These carts to and from London were able to keep running throughout the winter, unlike those to Coventry, which at that time had to suspend the service between the beginning of December and mid-March.[12] Legislation passed in 1631, giving Justices of the Peace powers to raise taxes for bridge upkeep, and in 1555, reiterating the local population's responsibility for the upkeep of 'the highways in their parish leading to any market town', may perhaps be seen to reflect the demands of increasing road traffic; and by the later sixteenth century there is clear evidence of heavier, four-wheeled wagons, as distinct from two-wheeled carts, travelling between London and such places as Canterbury, Norwich, Ipswich and Gloucester. In 1637 Taylor's *Carriers' Cosmographie*, which listed these departures from London, revealed that a remarkably extensive network of carriers was already in being, linking the capital

---

[10] L. C. A. Knowles, *The Industrial and Commercial Revolutions in Great Britain During the Nineteenth Century* (London, 1921), p. 236.
[11] C. H. Wilson, *England's Apprenticeship, 1603–1763* (London, 1965), p. 43.
[12] O. Coleman (ed.), *The Brokage Book of Southampton, 1443–4* (2 vols. Southampton, 1960, 1961); and 'Trade and prosperity in the fifteenth century: some aspects of the trade of Southampton', *Econ. Hist. Review*, XVI (1963), pp. 9–22.

with places as far away as York, Manchester and Exeter. This list and two later ones, in 1681 and 1715, have been studied by Dr Chartres who has produced what he calls a 'service quotient' to give some idea of the probable growth in freight traffic from London to various destinations between those years. According to his estimates and calculations, the number of services a week grew from 272 in 1637 to 610 in 1715, with wagons usually employed (he believes) for short and medium distances.[13]

This growing traffic put increasing pressure upon those rural parishes responsible for the upkeep of the major thoroughfares traversed by these heavy vehicles, each capable of carrying several tons of freight. In 1667, a ton and a half was allowed in the drier, summer months and by 1741 this had risen to three tons. Road hauliers always increase their profit by overloading; it is unlikely that they were more law abiding then, than those of more recent times. The local authorities argued, not unreasonably, that times had changed since most traffic was limited and local, and so was born the idea of the turnpike, to transfer the cost of upkeep of these main roads from the parish to the road users. At first this was done on instructions from the Justices of the Peace, but then other local worthies secured parliamentary sanction to set up a trust to accept responsibility.[14] A number of them became trustees, empowered to borrow up to a given amount for the improvement and upkeep of a stretch of road. The trustees were allowed to erect gates or bars at which the passing traffic paid tolls, on a published scale which varied according to the size of vehicle and type of traffic. The original hope was that the loan could be paid off by the end of the 21-year period covered by the Act. In practice, the cost of maintenance and the employment of toll collectors and other turnpike staff left the trust with a surplus sufficient only for the payment of the fixed interest on the loan. The trustees' later practice of auctioning toll collection and turnpike maintenance on an annual basis rendered the original goal even more remote. Turnpike Acts had to be renewed every time they ran out.

The first of these Turnpike Acts, passed in 1663, concerned a heavily trafficked stretch of the Great North Road near Hertford, 25 miles north of London. Tolls began to be collected in 1665, but this pioneer venture

[13]   J. A. Chartres, 'Road carrying in England in the seventeenth century: myth and reality', *Econ. Hist. Review*, February (1977), pp. 72–94. See also C. H. Wilson's 'Land carriage in the seventeenth century', and J. A. Chartres's response, 'On the road with Professor Wilson', *Econ. Hist. Review*, xxxiii (1980), pp. 92–9.
[14]   W. Albert, *The Turnpike Road System in England, 1663–1840* (Cambridge 1972), ch. 2.

had a chequered career and no tolls at all were collected between 1680 and 1690. The spread of turnpikes really began only in the early eighteenth century.[15] Dr Albert's painstaking study of the Acts of Parliament and the timing and location of the turnpikes to which they related has completely disproved the Webb's assertion that turnpiking was so piecemeal as to be ineffective. He shows that they were first adopted where the traffic was heaviest, on the main roads out of the capital, and were then introduced to these major routes farther afield. By 1750 the 13 main roads from London to places as far away as Berwick-on-Tweed on the Scottish border, Manchester, Chester, Hereford, Bristol and Portsmouth were all virtually completed.[16] Meanwhile a start had been made with the turnpiking of the busier stretches of road in industrializing areas. Many more of these link roads were improved and subject to toll during the years 1750 to 1770. Dr Eric Pawson, an historical geographer who has also made a study of this subject, has conveniently summarized the position in 1750 and 1770 on two maps, the latter showing a dense and impressive network as the interstices between the main roads came to be filled in.[17]

Although the days of the more scientifically minded road specialists, to whom the title 'engineer' could properly be applied, lay in the future, those carpenters, coal merchants, bakers, publicans and 'old infirm men' who were appointed surveyors by the turnpike trustees seem to have operated more effectively than their parish counterparts, who continued to be responsible for other roads in the parish as well as for making a limited statute labour or (later) financial contribution to the local turnpikes, too. Although Dr Albert concluded that the turnpike surveyors were for a long time 'barely adequate for their tasks', he nevertheless ultimately reached the conclusion that 'more ample resources permitted them to apply these traditional methods more intensively'.[18] In a recent essay he seems to take an even more favourable view of their activities:

> The minute and account books of the trusts show considerable attention not only to surfacing (the main repair activity) but also to improved drainage, widening, easing gradients, erecting markers and other improvements. The

---

[15] Ibid.

[16] Ibid., p. 189.

[17] E. Pawson, *Transport and Economy: The Turnpike Roads of Eighteenth Century Britain*, (London, 1977), pp. 140, 151. These maps have also been reproduced in: D. H. Aldcroft and M. J. Freeman (eds), *Transport and the Industrial Revolution* (Manchester, 1983), pp. 40, 43.

[18] Albert, *Turnpike Road System*, pp. 79, 167.

trustees may have had to rely on traditional practices until McAdam and Telford began to propagate more 'scientific' ideas (in the early nineteenth century), but at least they were able to employ them more intensively than the parish surveyors, and they were able to bring longer stretches of road under unified control. Moreover, they replaced unwilling and inefficient state labour with wage labour, and this probably increased the effectiveness of the old methods . . .[19]

It is clear that more heavily-loaded wagons were able to pass along the newly turnpiked roads. We have already seen that three-ton loads were allowed in the 1740s. By 1765 this was raised to six tons,[20] a weight greater than that carried by most motor lorries in the 1930s. Contemporary drawings and paintings depict these lumbering vehicles, piled high, lurching through the countryside. Even more significant perhaps is the evidence that fewer horses were needed to draw these greater tonnages. Seven per wagon had been allowed by law in 1662; only five in 1751.[21] Perhaps the special breeding of animals more suited to heavy haulage may explain some of this saving in costly horsepower, but the better roads must account for most of it. Falling freight charges during the eighteenth century, clearly indicated by assessments fixed by Justices of the Peace by an Act of 1691, confirm that the added cost of the numerous turnpike tolls was being more than offset by savings in horsepower per ton carried.[22] This was a vital gain which has been overlooked by earlier writers, who have concentrated instead on the broad wheel controversy – Parliament's insistence that these much heavier vehicles should fit nine-inch wheels, which would act as road rollers rather than rut-makers. 'Greater weights carried by fewer draught animals denotes a rise in efficiency of road transport and an increase in the productivity of capital invested in its facilities. In the light of this, the turnpike trusts established during the first half of the eighteenth century an important transport improvement in the economic sense,' Dr Albert concludes.[23]

According to the Chartres service quotient, the number of goods vehicles from London nearly doubled in the half century between 1715 and 1765. The number of vehicles was growing at a slightly faster rate than during the previous 79 years from 1637 to 1716. But, as might be expected with larger loads, the ton:mile estimates increased at a considerably faster rate between 1715 and 1765, more than sixfold, from an

[19] Albert in Aldcroft and Freeman, *Transport and the Indust. Rev.*, pp. 50–1.
[20] Albert, *Turnpike Road System*, p. 181.
[21] Ibid.
[22] Ibid., pp. 81, 260–2.
[23] Ibid., p. 181.

estimated total just over 13,000 to more than 80,000. From still quite small totals earlier in the century, the volume of road freight traffic between London and all parts of the country was growing impressively even before the Rostovian 'take-off'. The significance of the latter, however, is reflected in the subsequent far larger estimated ton:mileage figures: 136,000 in 1796, 375,000 in 1816 and 457,000 in 1840.[24]

Freight traffic along turnpike roads between other towns in the country was also on the increase during the eighteenth century, and feeder services were developed to connect with the main trunk hauliers at inns along their route, which served much the same function as railway goods depots were to do.[25] Nor must the contribution of local road freight transport be forgotten. This included heavy, bulky goods of low value, as well as the higher value freight which could stand the cost of road transport over longer distances, for much of the former had to be hauled by road over short distances to navigable water if bound for remote destinations, or to the local market town if intended for local sale. Even over longer journeys there were circumstances in which manufacturers or their agents might despatch their wares by water or by road, depending upon the urgency of delivery or the state of inland navigation in times of freezing or drought. Peter Stubs, for instance, the Warrington filemaker, delivered his specialized product in the later eighteenth century by canal, wagon or stage coach, as customers' requirements would seem to dictate.[26]

Passenger travel also developed rapidly during these years. Many people went by coastal ship, especially between England and Scotland, but very few seem to have been carried by inland waterway. For those who journeyed by road, horses were still available for hire and various forms of carriage too. Livery stables, increasing in number, provided these services and also, with inns along the road, were prepared to feed and water a traveller's own horses. These, however, were costly modes of travel, the equivalent of the hire car or private car nowadays. More important was the rapid growth of forms of public transport.

[24] J. A. Chartres and G. L. Turnbull, 'Road transport', in: Aldcroft and Freeman, *Transport and the Indust. Rev.*, p. 85. For an impressive, detailed study of a road haulier in this period, see the earlier part of G. L. Turnbull, *Traffic and Transport: An Economic History of Pickfords* (London, 1979).
[25] A. Everitt, 'The English urban inn, 1560–1760', in A. Everitt (ed.), *Perspectives in English Urban History* (London, 1973).
[26] T. S. Ashton, *An Eighteenth-Century Industrialist, Peter Stubs of Warrington, 1756–1806* (Manchester, 1939), ch. 7.

There were two: cheap, uncomfortable and relatively slow; or faster, less uncomfortable but quite expensive. The former involved travelling by the stage wagons which we have already mentioned. This, like the study of the livery stables, still awaits historical investigation. For the present, the lot of the humbler folk who rode on these laden goods vehicles can only be indicated by example, such as that of Elizabeth Strutt, then in her late twenties, who used this means to travel from Derby to London early in 1757. It took her three and a half days, including three overnight stops. The weather was wet and windy, and one day it snowed. On the first day, as she subsequently reported to her husband, 'I was so sick I was not able to travel further, but stayed behind ye waggon mor[e] than an hour, and then walked 5 miles before I came up with it.' Not surprisingly, she reached London after this trying experience with a very bad cold.[27]

Stage coaches, the more expensive form of passenger travel, date from the earlier seventeenth century. They were heavy vehicles, hardly cushioned at all against the constant jolting of the wheels. Yet the traffic grew. By the end of the century an observer was able to remark:

> England excels all other nations in the conveniency of stage coach services going at certain times to all parts of England, at least to the most noted places. Which is done with so much speed that some will reach 50 miles on a summer day; and at so easy rates that it is in some places less than a shilling for every five miles.[28]

Speeds of under five miles an hour were nothing to boast about; nor could a 10s. fare for a 50-mile journey be afforded by any but the better-off minority. Nevertheless at these speeds and fares a network was built up. More people were encouraged to travel.

The big acceleration in coaching was to come *not* with the improved surfaces of McAdam in the earlier nineteenth century, as is usually supposed, but in the third quarter of the eighteenth, thanks partly to turnpiking and greatly improved, sprung coaches, but mainly to better organization of the coach services, usually by the operator at the London end who organized the innkeepers along the route into a syndicate, giving them in return a share in the vehicle's profits. Each syndicate organized relays of horses along the route, the various teams being able to gallop at higher speeds over short distances of ten miles or so. Stops became briefer and coaches ran night and day so that passengers in a hurry could cut out

---

[27]   R. S. Fitton and A. P. Wadsworth, *The Strutts and the Arkwrights* (Manchester, 1958), pp. 27–8.
[28]   G. Miege, *The New State of England Under Our Present Monarch, King William III* (London, 1699), part 2, p. 22.

overnight stops altogether. (Those not so hard pressed could await the next day's coach.) Innkeepers came to depend more on their share in the coaches and less on food, drink and accommodation. Coaching inns were built which were better suited to meet these changing demands. The new 'flying machines', mounted on steel springs, cut the London–Manchester run between the early 1750s and the later 1780s (to take one not untypical example) from four and a half days – the old pace of under 50 miles a day with overnight stops – to about 28 hours. London–Newcastle was cut from six days to under two.[29]

Fares remained high, though they did not increase after 1750 as rapidly as did agricultural prices, including those for horse feed.[30] This relative fall in travelling costs, made greater by savings on overnight stops, was remarkable because the coaches had to meet not only the higher horsing costs, the turnpike tolls and other operating expenses, such as the depreciation of new or relatively new vehicles and regular servicing, but also from 1779 a mileage duty which was charged on the vehicle whether it ran full or empty. Each coach carried four or six passengers inside, protected from the elements, plus ten or so who shivered on the roof, fortified no doubt by their flask of ardent spirits, who only paid half as much. At the end of the 1750s, for instance, the single fare (inside) for the journey from Oxford to London, just under 60 miles, was 12s. 6d. and outside about 6s. (just over 1d. per mile). The much slower stage wagons then charged 3s. 6d.[31] At these rates, much larger coach traffics were developed on the routes out of London, especially after the mid-eighteenth century. The Chartres service quotient for passenger vehicles rises from an index number of 10 in 1715 to 18 in 1765, 24 in 1773 and 100 in 1796. His estimated number of passenger miles grows even more rapidly: from 67,000 (index number 10), to 123,000 (12), 183,000 (18) and 1,040,000 (100) in the same years.[32] Here is clear evidence of passenger transport responding to quickened economic growth by better organized traditional methods, without major technical change. Coach services between provincial towns were much less numerous earlier in the eighteenth century and were much slower to develop.[33] In several regions

---

[29]   W. T. Jackman, *The Development of Transportation in Modern England* (second ed. London, 1962), pp. 684–5, 691–2.
[30]   Pawson, *Transport and Economy*, p. 297.
[31]   Jackman, *The Development of Transportation*, p. 340 and appendix 6; Pawson, *Transport and Economy*, pp. 296, 298.
[32]   Chartres and Turnbull in Aldcroft and Freeman, *Transport and the Indust. Rev.*, p. 69.
[33]   Ibid., p. 69.

this accentuated coaching development in the industrial revolution period at the end of the century.

The coaches had been so accelerated by the 1780s that by then they travelled much faster than the Royal Mail, still carried on horseback by mature (and sometimes elderly) messengers who were known as post-boys. The Bath mail took nearly two days to come from London, whereas the coach managed the journey in half that time.[34] John Palmer, a Bath resident, persuaded the government to allow him as an experiment to carry the mail by coach between London and Bath, and to Bristol a little farther on (and 116 miles from London), with the same privileges and freedom from tolls as enjoyed by the postboys. The experiment was an outstanding success. The mail coach covered the distance reliably to and from Bath in 14 hours. It was the fastest vehicle on the road for it had right of way and, at the sound of the mail guard's blast on his post horn, all turnpike gates were thrown open for it to hurry through. Mail coaches were introduced on other routes. Their operators were able to charge their passengers (all inside) higher fares for this express service. Not only were the mails speeded up considerably; so were the newspapers, which then all went free by post having paid the stamp duty. The circulation of London papers was trebled in little over a decade.[35]

As population continued to grow after 1800 and economic activity quickened further, so the frequency of coach services was increased (sometimes by the stimulating arrival of a new competitor), and speeds were further improved, though not to the same extent as during the previous 50 years. Entrepreneurs, such as Edward Sherman and William Horne, emerged to take charge of organizing coach services on a much bigger scale from the London end and were soon major operators on a number of roads. It was at this juncture, with much larger turnpike takings resulting from the increase in traffic, that there came on the scene John L. McAdam, the much-publicized advocate of expenditure on road drainage and surfacing, and engineers like Telford, who built new stretches of road with reduced gradients and fewer bends, which also contributed to this further acceleration. After 1810 too, light sprung vans, capable of conveying three tons of goods, were put on the roads. These, also using relays of horses and running night and day, made a (largely successful) bid for some of the high value, category two traffic from the coaches at rates midway between those charged by coach and those by wagon. After 1814 Pickfords, for instance, soon built up a successful daily

---

[34]   H. Robinson, *Britain's Post Office* (Oxford, 1953), p. 104; Jackman, *The Development of Transportation*, p. 691.
[35]   Robinson, *Britain's Post Office*, p. 95.

service between London and Manchester which took 36 hours.[36] By 1821 the fastest coaches between London and Manchester were covering the 185 miles in 24 hours, only four fewer than in 1788. Nine years later this journey time had been cut to 20 hours, and in 1832 to 18.[37] An average speed of 10 miles per hour was perhaps the limit possible for vehicles drawn by horses. For any better performance mechanical power was needed.

This is the background to the application of steam power to transport. It was first used on colliery railways, previously horse-drawn, tentatively from 1805 and continuously from about 1810. Colliery engineers were accustomed to stationary steam engines and were only too willing to try to put them on wheels. They were rudimentary efforts, often too heavy for the track, and were always inefficient and slow; but coal was dirt cheap and speed was not needed.

In fact, the new steam transport technology was first used effectively not on land, but on boats in rivers and in coastal vessels. As Professor Bagwell has rightly claimed, the voyage made by the 75-ton paddle steamer *Thames* between 28 May and 12 June 1815, from Glasgow to London *via* Dublin, was as significant an event as the well-known Rainhill locomotive trials 14 years later.[38] Steam vessels were still carrying many passengers 40 years later. They also provided the railways with stiff competition on agricultural and coal traffic for much longer than that. They were still carrying a third or more of Aberdeen's livestock traffic to London even in the 1860s and 44 per cent of London's coal as late as 1870.[39]

Railways were nevertheless the epoch-making transport innovation from 1830, when the world's first inter-urban line was opened between Liverpool and Manchester. Their economic significance lay in their ability to handle both major categories of traffic, which no other single mode of transport had previously been able to do. They offered both lower cost and greater speed, though at first, and to everyone's utter surprise (as a result of the sudden and unexpected improvement of the Stephenson locomotive just before the Rainhill trials), the element of speed, which attracted passengers, mail and high value goods, proved

36   Turnbull, *Traffic and Transport*, p. 67.
37   Jackman, *The Development of Transportation*, pp. 699, 701.
38   P. S. Bagwell, *The Transport Revolution from 1770* (London, 1974), p. 65.
39   Ibid., p. 73; G. Channon, 'The Aberdeen beef trade with London: a study in steamship and railway competition, 1850–69', *Transport History*, March (1969), p. 5.

more important than the transport cost reductions on coal and other
category one traffic. Mails went to the new railway within six months of
its opening, and coaches running in direct competition with it swiftly lost
their clientele and were run off the road. The rival waterways, however,
having cut their rates and improved their services, continued to win traffic
for some years. A decade after the railway's opening, the volume of goods
carried by water between Liverpool and Manchester was more than twice
as great as that of its new competitor.[40]

Horse-drawn transport was by no means eclipsed by the steam railway
either. It is true, as we have seen, that coaches or other road vehicles
running in direct competition with trains had no hope of competing with
them, but it took time for the railway network to grow. Promotions of
the 'railway mania' of the mid-1840s completed the main skeleton, but
left many places remote from railways until branch lines were built in the
second half of the century. Even these branches never gave the country
full coverage. The railways in fact, by encouraging economic growth,
generated short-distance horse-drawn transport to and from railway
stations as well as encouraging local traffic within rural areas. Above all,
urbanization was proceeding apace and the rapidly growing towns relied
almost wholly upon horse-drawn vehicles for the movement of passengers and goods, apart from London and even there it is easy to exaggerate
the importance of suburban rail services and, from the 1860s, the
Underground.[41] According to Professor Thompson's estimates, there
were more horses involved in transport in Great Britain as a whole in
1851 (264,000) than there had been in 1811 (251,000). Even more
surprising this total grew throughout the railways' heyday, to over
1,100,000 in 1901.[42] The horse remained an increasingly familiar sight
upon Britain's roads and streets. The old and unmechanized proved a
remarkable survivor.

---

[40]   C. Hadfield and G. Biddle, *The Canals of North West England* (Newton
Abbot, 1970), vol. 1, p. 125.
[41]   T. C. Barker and M. Robbins, *A History of London Transport*, vol. 1
(London, 1963), chs 3, 6 and 8.
[42]   F. M. L. Thompson, 'Nineteenth-century horse sense', *Econ. Hist. Review*,
February (1976), p. 80.

6

Agriculture and Industrialization

Peter Mathias

The importance of agriculture in the process of economic change is such that it invites two sorts of inquiry. The first may be called the 'internal' or the intrinsic history of agricultural change and the second the 'external' relationships of agricultural developments as they interacted with processes of change more widely in the economy.

Agricultural change

Enclosures

Generalizations about enclosure being an absolute pre-condition for all agricultural improvement have recently become more qualified, more muted, with some local evidence (for example related to north Oxfordshire and Leicestershire) that unenclosed parishes did see some agricultural innovation in the seventeenth and eighteenth centuries. Certainly more flexibility existed in working the open fields than was previously supposed. This was particularly the case with new rotations on lighter soils; but it is doubtful whether turnips (as one key feature of 'Norfolk' innovations) were known on unenclosed land as a field crop. Individual cultivation and the management of beasts was still important for managing innovation, experimentation, the measurement of results, the control of costs, and the incentive structure required to bear the costs of innovation in prospect of enjoying its eventual rewards. The weight of tradition, the influence of the poorest cultivators, collective inertia, difficulties of getting agreement for change, problems of disease and improved breeding of animals were all maximized by the communal practices of common-field agriculture, with the collective pasturing of animals on commons, wastelands and open fields after the harvest.

The paramountcy of the enclosure movement (and with this the timing of agrarian change) has also been called into question by the awareness of its regional concentrations. Perhaps half the cultivated land of England was enclosed before the eighteenth century began, and some regions, such as much of Kent, and in the Celtic West had never known open fields. Much enclosure had taken place in the later seventeenth century and in the first half of the eighteenth century by agreement, without leaving traces in parliamentary evidence. This was easiest when one proprietor, or a small group, dominated agricultural land in a locality. Only 130 Parliamentary Enclosure Acts were on the statute book before 1760. One thousand were then passed during the next 40 years, covering seven million acres. This was the gross acreage, and included already enclosed patches of land within the superficial area of the awards.

The incentive to seek enclosure through the parliamentary process of a private act (which was also the legal form under which most transport investment in turnpike roads, canals and subsequently railways took place) came where leading proprietors could not easily get agreement without such legal powers to overcome reluctant minorities. The costs of enclosure awards also increased with the numbers of those entitled to share in the distribution. Hence parliamentary enclosures increased, as incentives for extending and intensifying cultivation rose with the steady trend rise in agricultural prices after 1750. Enclosures were not simply to facilitate the conversion of arable to pasture land, although some conversion may have characterized regional specialization developing in the first half of the eighteenth century, with the fall in cereal prices offering better returns, where soil and markets suited, from grazing. This was probably the case in Midlands counties such as Leicestershire, for example. But parliamentary enclosures in the second half of the century were prominent in the corn-growing east, east Midlands and north-east, and where grain-growing was associated with 'mixed' or 'convertible' husbandry – integrated with the management of stock.

Enclosure, when associated with agricultural innovation, was important for increasing the effectively farmed cultivated area. Farms were created from empty land, moorland, woodland, common land, and fenland, which was divided up and brought into regular cultivation. The pre-enclosure economies of such localities, with the pattern of local communities, were viable – often economically effective and socially prosperous – on their own terms; but with a much smaller local population and labour force relative to the area and a much less intensive use of land; for example through summer grazing, fishing, fowling, reed-gathering and the like in the Fens and an equivalent mix of operations in other contexts. As much as two million acres were taken from 'wastes' in the eighteenth century, with further large inroads during the Napoleonic Wars, when scarcity prices made it profitable to cultivate very poor upland soils.

Apart from extending the cultivated area, from land which previously had never been under the plough, in a regular succession of straw crops – probably the most important single effect of the enclosure movement in stimulating agricultural output – enclosure, in association with the new rotations, had a similar effect in increasing the net amount of land under cultivation by eliminating the fallow year, through winter feed crops and nitrogenous grasses (clover, lucerne and sain-foin). The net effect of the agricultural changes coming after enclosure led towards more intensive farming practice. Improved organization was itself one source of increasing agricultural productivity. The eighteenth century saw a gradual increase in the average size of farm in certain regions (sometimes off-set in the averages by the increase in the number of small-holdings for specialist crops such as hops or market gardens and fruit). Such consolidation, where it occurred, was also consequential upon the process of enclosure, which in extending the rights of ownership thereby facilitated alienation and a more active land market at the local level. Consolidation of farms could also come, of course, from the action of landlords throwing farms together and eliminating some tenancies, without equivalent change in the freeholds.

Agricultural innovations

The timing of the introduction of all the classic innovations has also been pushed back a long way – to a seventeenth-century 'agricultural revolution'.[1] The classic dating, it is now apparent, was following the 'showmen', the noble publicists, not the innovators representative of the

---

[1] The very thoroughly documented work of Dr Eric Kerridge has undoubtedly been primarily responsible for this. The issue is still not without its complications, however. There may now be many known instances where new techniques date from the mid or early seventeenth century rather than the eighteenth. This does not by itself authenticate such individual instances as *representative* of farm practice in those regions. Statistical significance is given not so much by the aggregate number of individual citations, but by the proportion which such instances of innovation bear to the whole area in question. Sampling techniques or detailed local studies could take the proof one stage further if systematic data allow.

original spread of new farm practices but rather when the aristocracy and the fashionable found out what was going on and cashed in on it. This is true of Bakewell on breeding techniques, Lord Townshend on turnips (which were possibly not so uniquely important in comparison with the other winter feed crops and grasses) or Coke in the Norfolk rotations.

The earliest changes came to rotations and the increasing flexibility in the use of land, particularly through 'ley' farming or 'up-and-down' convertible husbandry, which employed temporary grass 'leys', sheep folding and the plough in various rotations. This was also associated very early, in the early seventeenth century if not before, with the use of nitrogenous grasses which helped to maintain fertility by 'fixing' nitrogen in the soil, as well as providing feed (and hence more fertility from the dung of animals they fed). It is the spread of these practices in Midland counties during the seventeenth century which puts them ahead of the process of enclosure in many localities. Turnips became a field crop in Suffolk for the first time, it seems, in the mid-seventeenth century, and spread outwards from there, but following enclosure, to provide more substantive winter-feed for stock, with other less publicized roots such as swedes and mangel-worzels. Innovations in crops and rotations jointly meant the chance of eliminating the normal one-in-three fallow year for straw crops.

Recent research has also revealed a wider range of responsiveness to technical and market opportunities in the seventeenth century: specialist crops such as hops, vegetables, fruit, dyestuffs, even tobacco in the early part of the century; and the 'floating' of watermeadows to give earlier springtime grazing. In-breeding techniques also spread to farm animals from dogs and racehorses in Restoration England. The redating of innovation over crops and rotations is coupled with a paradoxical view about the slowness of diffusion of the new innovations, particularly the new implements, the horse-drawn hoes and lighter iron ploughs, which were still marching across the land, generally in the direction of the west and north-west, in the early nineteenth century. John Marshall, one of the shrewdest observers, said in 1794 that there was not a pair of wheels to be seen on a farm in Devonshire. The innovations of new crops and rotations, on the other hand, spread more rapidly, where the soil and climate were suitable. The concept of 'revolution', implying a fast pace of change, is thus an even greater misnomer for agriculture than for industry. The dynamics of innovation in agriculture are removed from a few heroic individuals and seen to be very much more diffused, very much more anonymous, very much more responsive to farm environment and economic context than in the older books where they are treated as the achievement of a handful of archetypes – aristocrats, leisured cranks like Jethro Tull, or the publicists like Arthur Young. This represents a fairly typical revaluation whenever the process of technical change and innovation has been analysed in detail.

Tenant farmers – substantial men on large farms – were the real leaders. The landlord actively initiating innovation by writing improvement clauses into his leases, and seeking to force capital investment upon his tenants, was not representative. The landowner was almost never, by analogy, the managing director of the enterprise, nor even usually its part-time chairman, but simply the main shareholder. Effective leasehold was important but the much advocated longer leases without intermediate rent-reviews, which were designed to give tenant farmers an incentive to make productive investment on the farm using their own capital, did not predominate. James Caird was still complaining about the rarity of such leases in the 1850s. Evidently rack rents were widely acceptable as a vehicle for reasonable relationships between landlord and farmer.

An effective steward or agent was an important advocate for improvement on the landlord's behalf. Apart from the essential business of collecting rents, the landlord depended on his steward for getting efficient tenants, seeking to encourage their efficiency, and at the same time keeping them reasonably content, a difficult intermediary role to play successfully. But the fact that large tenant farmers were the key to improvement (more than small proprietors) does underline the significance of leasehold tenures. Land-use clauses in leases – preventing manure from being sold off the farm and controlling sequences of straw crops – were probably used by landlords to maintain the capital value of their farms, at least to prevent abuse where necessary, more than to enforce improvement on a wide scale. They were primarily defensive in intent. Tenant farmers, on larger farms in particular, were not simply creatures of a landlord's will or whim and are by no means to be considered as a 'down-trodden', subservient, inert group. Considerable capital was required to equip, stock and work a farm; and considerable expertise needed to keep it profitable and in good heart. A landlord greatly depended upon his tenant farmers for their capital and expertise. The worst fate for a landlord was to have his lands untenanted – taking land in hand was a usual formula for losing money – and this would be likely to happen if a landlord made unreasonable demands upon his tenant farmers, in good times as well as bad (when some rent might have to be remitted). The absence of formal evidence probably does less than justice to the constructive results which the initiatives of a vigorous steward (and increasing rents) could have in inducing tenants to improve.

The land market seems to have become very restricted at the end of the eighteenth century, with a steep rise in the price of land. Where the landlord provided fixed capital and the tenant put his own savings into stock and equipment, in areas of larger units of land-ownership and farms, farmers could not use their profits for buying more land, particularly where immediately adjacent land was not available. Greater incentives were therefore developed to improve stock and invest capital in productive ways on farms. Leasehold also allowed the consolidation of farms to occur more easily, without bankruptcy, and other responses necessary for raising agricultural efficiency and thus also rents.

New generalizations have also been made about the process of innovation itself, apart from its timing. The leading edge of innovations lay to the eastern side of the country, Norfolk, Suffolk, Lincolnshire, Northumberland, the eastern side of Scotland being the strategic regions – all areas of large farms. The innovations were slowest to penetrate in the west: Devon, Cornwall, Wales, the north-west Highlands. This was partly a question of soil and climate, no doubt, but these areas were also characterized by a very much more fragmented pattern of holdings and small proprietorships.

Innovations were concentrated on light land with sandy or chalky soils, more than on the heavy clays. Stiff, wet clay lands responded more to drainage in the nineteenth century (expensive undersoil conduits) than to Enclosure Acts in the late eighteenth century. So much of the logic of the technical innovations, whether the logic of crops like barley, or a higher level of stocking of sheep or folding sheep on land to maintain fertility in 'ley' rotations, was that of well-drained, lighter soils, not stiff, heavy, wet clays. Not coincidentally, most of the recorded responsiveness of open field farming was also on the lighter soils.

During the French wars enclosures were concentrated in Lincolnshire, Yorkshire, Norfolk and Cambridge. Berkshire, Wiltshire, Somerset and Gloucester formed a secondary area heavily enclosed in this period. There were 246 Enclosure Acts in the 1780s, 469 in the 1790s and 847 in the decade 1800–1809. They followed the pull of higher grain prices on trend, but the swings of money-market conditions and credit facilities in the short run (apart from 1796/7). A steep rise came in wartime: in 1793–1804 1.5 million acres were enclosed, under 921 Acts. These wartime enclosures pushed into land which was marginal under eighteenth-century techniques – uplands, moors, lakeland fells and fens. Wartime developments also shifted towards labour-economizing techniques as wages rose, with a rush of patents for innovations like reapers and threshers. In the event, threshing machines proved the only important successful response and these affected only the post-harvest peak of labour requirements. Threshing machines also spread along the traditional route from east to west. Was this great spread of arable cultivation during the French wars at the expense of meat supplies? As the commons disappeared did numbers of livestock rise on arable land? The enforced complementarity of stock and crop farming, especially on light soils, makes a fall in numbers of livestock (particularly sheep) doubtful, although buying for the armed forces, concentrated in the south of England may have reduced civilian supplies, as prices rose in wartime. The main stagnation of meat supplies relative to population growth probably came rather earlier in the eighteenth century. Meat prices were maintained, but there was no growing differential with corn prices in the latter part of the century. Much extra bad land went under the plough, but not seriously at the expense of stock.

The Board of Agriculture

The Board of Agriculture was established by Pitt in 1793 as part of the campaign to extend home food supplies. Arthur Young became its secretary at £400 per annum. It proved a typical piece of rather bumbling, amateur, resource-starved eighteenth-century English administration, not at all a department of state in the sense of administering policy. Its closest parallel today would be a farmer's advice bureau, set up to survey the state of farming across the country, to discover the extent of waste land, unimproved farming practices and the like. As a whole the Commissioners represented the landed oligarchy not the farmers; it was more in the style of the Country Landowners' Association than the National Farmers' Union. The Board had no executive power to effect change. It institutionalized a rather amateur hobby of the English landed classes and, characteristic of amateurs, its reports were very mixed in quality, much of the data being supplied by local parsons. Its publicity seems to have been more useful to historians than contemporaries. Apart from the publication of reports, the main objective of the Board in 1793 was to press for a general Enclosure Act to cheapen the process of enclosure (a great ambition of the gentry and farm interest), which was accepted by Parliament in the wake of famine prices in 1801, after various committees of enquiries.

This Act was a shadow of what it might have been. Average costs of enclosure, involving an individual Act of Parliament with full parliamentary process, fees and legal expenses for each local project were very high – creating a pressing burden, particularly on smaller landholders. Only about a quarter of the expense actually went on the fences and hedges, the rest being absorbed in surveying costs and fees of various kinds. Average costs varied from a few shillings to a few pounds per acre. Oxfordshire costs were low at 27s. 6d. per acre in the 1780s. The Board of Agriculture thought average costs were 38s. 6d. per acre in the early 1790s and they had reached 40s. per acre by 1800. Because parliamentary and other fees did not increase proportionately with the scale of the project (unlike fencing costs), the burden upon small projects was relatively greater. Costs were also greater where the number of proprietors was highest. Hence the 'open field' smallholders bore the greatest burdens and the areas dominated by large numbers of small cultivators were on the 'trailing edge' of the process of enclosure. The smallholders were thus subject to double pressure: they had smaller savings, less access to credit than larger landowners and they needed more capital per acre, to survive the process of enclosure.

The object of a General Enclosure Act was to standardize the forms and processes sufficiently to be able to decentralize these legal procedures from Westminster to local magistrates, cutting out all the expenses involved with shepherding a bill through Parliament. It turned out to be a dismal half measure because it ran up against the two prime vested interests of eighteenth-century England – clerics defending their tithes and lawyers defending their fees. Despite all the thrust of the parliamentary reports and well-rehearsed dialogues with compliant legal witnesses produced as evidence, the General Enclosure Act of 1801 proved a very hollow triumph, after which the Board of Agriculture ceased to command such confidence amongst the farming community.

Agricultural change and rural protest

To affirm the increase in employment generated in agriculture and an absence of food shortages (apart from the short-term problems of bad harvests and wartime emergencies) is not to imply that changes came to rural society without stress or outbreaks of violence. Protests were prompted, in part, by the changes in status – the depression in status as it was assumed – and against accepting the fate of becoming farm labourers, occasioned by the withdrawal of rights of use over land, or a conventional title to land.

This was arguably as much a cultural protest as it was a consequence of a deterioration of material well-being, low as the money rewards of the agricultural labourers were in eighteenth-century England. They certainly formed, collectively, the lowest-paid social group in the country (apart from the domestic servants) as well as much the largest. If ever there was relevance in the concept of a 'reserve army' of labour it was here, long antedating the urban factory economy. In the most purely agricultural regions of the country, the south, the south-west and Wales, wage levels were at their lowest, and material satisfactions at their bleakest. It was in the agricultural south that the incidence of pauperism was at its highest at the end of the eighteenth and in the early nineteenth century. In other, more rapidly developing regions, agricultural wages were rather higher, being set by the higher rates of pay available in alternative employment, but everywhere a similar differential existed between wages on and off the land. The doubt is simply that the status of peasant, or a title to land, or traditional rights of use over land, did not by itself ensure any higher standard of reward. Indeed, in the early nineteenth century, the worst examples of penury and rural squalor lay in the peasant areas of Ireland, central Wales and the north-west Highlands. Most peasants paid rent.

Social protest was not marked by persistent endemic violence in rural England. Food riots in towns were much more prevalent. In countries with a two-deck structure of rural society – landowners and a peasantry – the mark of rural violence *in extremis* was burning chateaux and the destruction of rent-rolls, because the landowner was seen as the oppressor. In England the farmer, as the employer, experienced confrontation with the farm labourers. Country houses, or Oxford or Cambridge colleges, did not burn. But flaming ricks were also very seldom seen. Agrarian violence, as in 1755–6, 1765–6, 1795, 1816 or particularly in 1830–1, or 1838–9 in Wales, did flare up on occasion, expressed against traditional medieval enemies like the middleman – miller or grain merchant – or against new technology such as the threshing machines, or against symbols of the new market economy like the turnpikes gates. But this was very limited, compared with almost any other country known, and a reaction (it might be claimed) more to the crises of the short-term – the bad harvest, scarcity food prices, high unemployment, that came and went within the year or within a couple of seasons – than to the structural logic associated with new social relationships in rural society and agriculture. Rural violence had been more prevalent in previous times in England, and in other countries with other forms of agrarian structure. Historians of rural society have been too much concerned with the niceties of tenurial relationships and the assumed social evils of the disappearance of the peasant and the yeoman. The danger signals of this tradition have been seen in romanticizing their role in history. This is a luxury which only a national heritage without a depressed peasantry has been able to afford.

Agriculture and the economy

The connections between agriculture and economic development fall under four headings: food supplies; the relationship between factors of production in agriculture and in other sectors of the economy; the income effects of agricultural changes; and demand created by the farm sector. The scale of resources involved in agriculture, by labour force, by share of the national income, by sources of savings in the economy, by the extent of national demand for its staple products, made agricultural developments crucial in the process of growth – if not as a motor of growth initiating the impetus for economic change, then as an 'enabling condition' which prevented constraints throttling the impetus developing elsewhere in the economy. More than a third of the national income still derived directly from agriculture at the end of the eighteenth century (more if indirect linkages are included) and over a third of the labour force were still in farming. On the demand side perhaps three-quarters of an unskilled labourer's weekly wage was spent in buying food and drink for his family. Moreover this was the most inelastic form of demand – basic food buying was necessary however high prices rose – so that fluctuations in the price of agricultural products were the most important single influence upon the level of home demand, and such prices fluctuated year by year according to the harvest more widely than any other major category of product.

Labour supplies

The factors potentially released from agriculture were labour, capital and enterprise. The story of enclosing landlords being the capitalist press-gang, driving labour off the land into industry and non-agricultural employment was denied by most informed contemporaries at the time and has finally been ruled out of court, at least in its simplest, direct form, by J. D. Chambers and other modern scholars. As Sir John Sinclair wrote to his fellow members of the Board of Agriculture in 1794:

> it has been urged that the improvement of wastes [i.e. enclosure] has a tendency to depopulate the country by diminishing the number of Cottagers, who ... in a great measure, exist, as it is supposed, by the miserable profits derived from them. Such an idea, however, is as little justified by experience, as it is evidently contrary to reason and common sense. It is impossible to suppose that the poor should be injured by that circumstance, which secures to them a good market for their labour (in which the real riches of a Cottager consists) which will furnish them with the means of constant employment ...[2]

---

[2]   Appendix B, *Report from the Select Committee on the Cultivation of Wastelands*, Parliamentary Papers, p. 204.

Sir Frederick Eden, who did not miss an opportunity of enlarging upon the springs of poverty, wrote in the same generation: 'Deserted villages in Great Britain are only to be found in the fictions of poetry. Our agricultural parishes are better stocked now than they were one hundred years ago when ... the visionary evils ascribed to the existence of commercial and agricultural capitalists did not exist.' The reasons, laid out by Professor Chambers, and confirmed by census reports which indicate gradually rising labour inputs for agriculture until 1851, are clear. Between 1811 and 1831 the number of families recorded as engaged in agriculture rose from 896,000 to 961,000. After a change in the categories, which makes exact comparisons impossible, the 1841 census reported 1,434,000 males engaged in agriculture and the 1861 census 1,779,000 males in agriculture. Given the slow, but steady increase in population during the first half of the century, in a context of rising agricultural exports, agricultural output was rising – it is now thought by at least 6 per cent per decade in the period 1700–60, just under 5 per cent per decade in 1760–1800, and at almost 12 per cent per decade in 1800–31. Innovations affecting agricultural techniques in the eighteenth century increased overall the cultivated area, and the productivity per acre, by increasing the intensity of use of land, more than they increased productivity per head of the agricultural labour force. This generalization is fundamental to understanding the impact of agrarian change. Everywhere the trend was to a more intensive use of land, higher annual values of output of grain and stock, with eventually higher rents for landlords.

Techniques improving output per head of the labour force did not advance with comparable strides. Certain gains came, not so much from improvements in technique, but from a better organization of the labour force. Squatters with rights of use over little land had low productivity because of underemployment, being idle in farming much of the time and seeking to eke out their living in other ways, often equally marginal. Agricultural labourers employed on larger enclosed farms had more work to do; so that a rise in productivity could come from the reorganization of farmland alone. The period shows certain other trends implying improved organization of labour; a trend, before the French wars at the end of the century, from owner-occupiers to leasehold tenants; from those with rights of use over land to tenant farmers and labourers; towards a gradual consolidation of farms as some large estates were built up, or as smallholders unable to bear the capital costs of enclosure sold out. But many great estates were built up without any appreciable effects upon the size of farms or their improvement – tenants simply changed landlords. Moreover the process of enclosure during the period of high wartime prices saw a halt to the squeeze put upon the smallholders, the owner-occupiers. With high prices for their products and optimistic country bankers, they could remain viable more easily than before 1790 or after 1815. In the great extension of the cultivated area coming from the attack on wastes and commons, small owner-occupiers, large landowners and tenant farmers all gained.

Beyond this increased efficiency in the use of labour, some improvement in technique also operated in the same direction. Light iron implements, particularly the 'Rotherham' plough, reduced labour costs and draught animals (which were also labour-intensive); but these spread on light soils more than heavy soils and were part of the process of increasing new acreage under the plough from old pastoral areas, so the net effect may well have been to increase labour inputs overall. The new iron implements, such as the seed-drill also spread very slowly. The major innovation of a labour-releasing kind came only at the end of the century, diffusing rapidly during the war years when money wages were rising rapidly in agriculture. This was mechanized threshing and chaff-cutting. But threshing took place in the autumn months following the harvest and the basic techniques of harvesting, which created the peak seasonal demand for labour, remained almost untouched by innovations. With labour inputs set by the peak requirements (even if supplemented by women's and children's work at harvest time) there was reduced incentive to employ labour-releasing innovations at other times of the year on the farm. Agricultural expansion thus involved an expanding labour force throughout this period, even though productivity per head was rising, and even though the agricultural labour force was declining steadily after 1770 as a percentage of total occupied population. Even this relative decline must be considered a moot point during the years of maximum enclosure during the French wars.

There has been much investigation of the balance between population, labour in agriculture and migration between enclosed and non-enclosed parishes in the eighteenth century. Some results suggest that the open-field agriculture in some areas (particularly on light soils in the Midlands) did see innovations and also that more labour was held in agriculture there than in enclosed parishes. This, however, is a secondary, and relative point. Overall, there is no doubt that, during the industrial revolution, indeed up to the mid-nineteenth century, agriculture in Britain expanded absolutely in output and required more labour inputs to do so, even though this happened very gradually.

The argument does not rest there, however. This is to speak, of course, of absolute numbers employed and absolute output rather than the *relative* shares of the labour force and contribution to gross domestic product. Clearly, the economy and the labour force were experiencing great relative change, with a structural transformation away from agriculture towards other sectors of the economy. In absolute terms the agricultural sector was growing slowly, as was the labour force; while in relative terms both were declining steadily. Much local migration did occur in late eighteenth-century England from the *increase* in numbers born primarily in a rural setting. The migration flows, although on a local rather than an inter-regional scale, were from an agricultural context to non-agricultural employment: from land to industry, to port, to urban work, to coalfield, and – such being the relative state of technique at the time, and the relative state of the labour market – this was a transfer from areas of low productivity, of marginal labour, to areas of higher productivity; from an area where diminishing returns were most likely with additional labour (beyond a certain point) to areas with increasing returns. Such local migration, and such transfers to non-agricultural employment, were much affected by the structure of rural society in Britain, in contrast to Ireland. Universal access to land did not exist; landlords were not willing to subdivide holdings to accommodate new families pressing for settlements. Extra numbers, beyond the employment available from expanding agriculture, had to sustain themselves by non-agricultural employment, either by local migration or by 'putting-out' work spreading through these rural regions of increasing population density. Often in England the nailing stint, the loom or the stocking frame became a substitute for the potato patch in Ireland or the north west Highlands. The structure of rural society, that is to say, helped to ensure that rising numbers did not multiply as a largely subsistence peasantry, in the sector of the economy with lowest productivity and diminishing returns. Thus, if enclosure did not create an industrial labour force by rural depopulation, the agrarian structure equally resisted the incentives towards sub-division and subsistence agriculture that population pressure might have produced. Most of the *increment* in rural population did not find employment in agriculture.

Capital

The contribution that agriculture made to economic growth by way of capital and credit links was as much a consequence of social relationships and attitudes as it was a question of economic and technical considerations. The net direction of such flows cannot be measured – varying seasonally and between long-term and short-term movements – but the strong tides moving in both directions could give mutual sustenance, and are evidence of the vigour of economic flows in Britain, the responsiveness to commercial opportunities and pressures. Their potential importance is to be measured by the fact that Gregory King thought that more than half the savings being created in the economy were flowing from farmers' profits and landowners' rents (more the aggregate of 'gentlemen's' rents than those of the peers). Primarily this was of significance for productive investment in agriculture itself. Given the technical and market opportunities available it was important that farmers and landowners should invest productively to improve the efficiency of farming, not just to buy more land – the classic response of the peasant with savings. Leasehold, the representative form of land tenure in England, had certain advantages in this respect. The farmer was more tempted to put capital into productive assets, implements and stock, if he could not buy his farm. Larger landowners had better access to capital for mortgages than smaller cultivators or peasants (and this became one of the best organized capital markets in the country in the late seventeenth and eighteenth century, both in London and at the local level). Landlord capital was the main instrument for 'fixed' investment in agriculture, in buildings and those forms of improvement which enhanced the capital value of the farm, such as drainage or enclosure, the tenant being responsible for implements, seeds and stock. It was also easier to consolidate farms and to organize improvements that needed large-scale decisions (as for fen drainage enclosure) where the larger landlord could enforce such decisions on tenants, than where large numbers of independent small proprietors were in possession and collective agreement was a pre-condition for change, at least in the absence of state pressure.

Larger landowners could take such decisions over the heads of their tenants, and effective leasehold tenure also allowed a change of cultivator without a change of owner, so that the inefficient cultivator could be removed more easily. And for many landlords by the eighteenth century, their estates encumbered with mortgages that fixed entail and strict settlement made it easier to obtain, farm improvement followed by increased rents was the hope of salvation. Hence also at least one of the incentives to develop mineral leases, and to finance canals and turnpikes which might bring the farms on their estates within the range of urban food markets – which might yield a better income to their tenant farmers and eventually higher rents for themselves. This is not to say that the English landed classes failed to indulge in their full share of non-productive conspicuous expenditure, whether building as grandly as their incomes (or the limits of a mortgage) allowed in the country, or spending lavishly in London or on the Continent. One is simply saying that it seems they also put more money into productive investment than most landed classes in other countries. In England, the opportunities for such commercial exploitation of their fortunes was greater than in most other regions in Europe, as well as their own inclinations and values being more responsive to them.

Some of the most vigorously improving landlords, like the Cokes of Holkham, ploughed back up to 20 per cent of their rents in improvements; but the more usual level, even for famous families such as the Bedfords or the Townshends, was 10 per cent or below. Landlord capital was also important in mining investment in many areas. The stewards of landowners such as the Fitzwilliams, Ravensworths or the Londonderrys (or even the Bishop of Durham) became virtually the departmental managers of great mining concerns. Even if the actual mining operations were usually leased out in concessions, some of the strategy of development as well as much of the capital came from the landlords. And in the eighteenth century a certain number of the operations were kept in hand. In Cornwall much landlord capital went into copper and tin mining, where shareholding spread capital investment very widely. Cornish china-clay development, although on a much smaller scale originally than tin or copper mining, with smaller capitals engaged and much lesser men therefore able to enter the trade, became a similar tale in the late eighteenth century. In mining, country landowners were very far from being 'mere' landed gentry or 'Corn Law lords'. The most successful cartel in coal-mining was run from the House of Lords by the landed magistrates of the north-east coast.

Equally a strong flow of landlord capital supported transport investment, canals and turnpikes, or urban development (less directly 'productive' investment). Individual opposition, of course, occurred, whether against the precise route of a scheme or against a rival venture which might reduce the profitability of one's investment in a certain project but, on the whole, landowning capital profoundly influenced the transport booms. The most detailed analysis made of shareholding in canal companies in the period 1760–1815 has shown that the landed classes contributed just under one third of the total – almost all coming from landlord groups rather than tenant farmers.[3] This is perhaps, not as great a proportion as some generalizations have suggested, but it is certainly not negligible. Moreover the support of landowners for a venture could well prove more important strategically than their share of the subsequent capital might suggest. Although the main initiators and organizers of such schemes tended to be the businessmen, industrialists and merchants hoping to profit directly, the political influence of landed proprietors was such that their opposition to the parliamentary bill could block a scheme.

[3]   J. R. Ward, *The Finance of Canal Building in Eighteenth-Century England* (Oxford, 1974).

Where they were known to be committed to support of a bill its chances were much improved. Landowners' motives were mixed – the desire to improve the access of their lands to urban markets, or for receiving supplies of lime, fuel and manure. Capital values as well as current income were at stake. They looked for profit directly as investors and also sought to maintain local leadership and influence in the county if such a project had the backing of their tenants.

Direct sponsorship of industrial enterprise was less representative of landlord interests by the end of the eighteenth century; while actual farming was the business of tenants. In no sense were the large British estates units of agricultural production like the great *latifundia* of east Prussia. Most aristocratic model farms, like their kitchen gardens and hot-houses, were not commercial propositions. Landowers wanted the finest farm animals, just as they wanted the fastest horses, for prestige rather than for profits. This is not to say that they were uninfluential in other ways but, compared with the earlier part of the eighteenth century, it seems that by its end landlords had taken a step back from the direct promotion and control of production enterprise. Even in land improvement the main weight of advance came from the large, wealthy tenant farmers, men of means and substance farming 200 acres and above; the men Arthur Young called the 'great farmers'.

Of course the land also gave forth its sons, and its capital, in the steady flow of younger sons taking their patrimony and themselves off the estate to other careers (mainly in the professions, particularly the Army and Navy) in traditional style. But, in turn, the land welcomed with wide embrace the successful merchants and industrialists returning to become country gentlemen with their accumulated profits: Richard Arkwright in Herefordshire, Samuel Oldknow near Mellor, the Marshalls of Leeds in the Lake District, every known London brewer (not infrequently on good barley land) in that great, traditional process of social metabolism which was characteristic of the English landed classes. Such landed families were 'open-ended at both ends': the younger sons being pushed off the family estates at the same time as landed society received recruits from the professional and commercial classes. Some doubts have been cast recently by Lawrence Stone on the 'openness' of this élite and the degree of social mobility evinced by newcomers to English landed society in the eighteenth century and the nineteenth century, taking support for the latter century also from the research of William Rubinstein in *Men of Property*.[4] However Stone and Rubinstein make extreme demands in

[4]   W. Rubinstein, *Men of Property. The Very Wealthy in Britain since the Industrial Revolution* (London, 1981); L. Stone and J. C. F. Stone, *An Open Elite? England 1540–1880* (Oxford, 1984).

their definition of social mobility – Stone counting only access to the ranks of the very largest landowning and country houses, and Rubinstein only access to the ranks of the millionaires – and in a single generation. I do not think this subverts the traditional generalizations about social mobility and the openness of the English landed élite at lower levels than the very tip of the pyramid.

It is impossible to say whether the capital flowed more in one direction than another in such investment. Landed estates were carrying a very heavy burden of mortgage debt in the eighteenth century, much of it supposedly raised from professional and commercial sources, supplementing the dowries brought to the land by the heiress daughters of merchants. Dr P. G. M. Dickson has documented another flow within this mortgage market: the insurance premiums moving into London-based insurance companies, like the Sun Fire Office, from merchants and industrialists, were creating balances usually put into the mortgage market for landowners and farmers.[5] A large number of smaller transfers out of land by young men must be balanced against these transfers back, mainly in later life, which could be on a spectacular scale. Richard Arkwright's Hampton Court Estate in Herefordshire, for example, which cost him £229,000 equalled nearly 60 per cent of the total annual investment of fixed capital in the entire cotton industry in 1809. The yield of those investments in land was much lower than comparable investments in trade or industry – the 'psychic' income making up the balance, compounded of security, political influence, prestige and pleasure.

The balance sheet of this possible net 'haemorrhage' of capital contains one or two additional items. Such investments in land commonly brought with them attitudes of profit calculation, productive investment, 'plough-back' learned in trade and industry. The Arkwrights and Oldknows of the farming world were improving landlords, as Adam Smith thought such recruits to the landed classes were as a group, in contrast to the 'mere' landed gentry. And, looking at the process from the point of view of the firm, when crisis struck or when a leap forward in investment proved very 'lumpy' in the demands it made for capital, freehold land and property was the best possible security for raising cash in the mortgage market. But E. L. Jones concludes his discussions of the Arkwright estates: 'the opportunity costs of land purchases like that of Hampton Court were high. Economic growth could surely have come faster without them.'[6] The conclusion remains that flows both ways, to and

[5]   P. G. M. Dickson, *The Sun Insurance Office, 1710–1960* (London, 1960), pp. 244 *et seq.*
[6]   E. L. Jones and G. E. Mingay (eds), *Land, Labour and Population in the Industrial Revolution* (London, 1967), p. 71.

from the land, suggest a responsiveness to commercial opportunity and financial advantage as well as to the dictates of social status.

The great expansion in agriculture in the final decade of the eighteenth century and up to the fall in prices in 1814 may mean that this sector was sucking in more capital resources than it was releasing – although the great rise in prices and profits enabled *both* great expansion of agriculture and a release of savings to other sectors, more particularly into government debt, because of the great decanting of purchasing power into the hands of farmers and landlords from the food-consumers, with a shift from internal levels of consumption towards savings by the mechanism of higher food prices.

So far we have been considering the one-to-one connections between landlord families and capital flows. To this must be added the institutional connection once a country banking system had spread through most rural areas and had begun to tap the savings of the 'farm' sector – that is, when deposit banking encouraged farm profits and landlords' rents to come to rest in the banking system, rather than in the iron chest or under the mattress. Banking deposits activated hoards and idle balances. A banker lived, as he still lives, on margins, and so was forced to employ funds at greater profit than the interest he had to pay to depositors. Hence bankers had to look for profitable – and safe – means of putting the deposits of customers to work. This flow from the land to the banking system was not very important until the end of the eighteenth century and it may well have consisted of farm profits more than landed surpluses. So many estates were burdened with mortgages that which way the credit flowed is a moot point. Perhaps the main directions of long-term credit flows were towards the land, with mortgage debt, while short-term credit flows were more from the land to the seasonal financing of trade and industry. The direction of short-term credit flows became significant at the end of the century, as well as being then on a sharply rising scale. The movement went from the agricultural areas of East Anglia and the eastern side of the country, the south and the south-west – undergoing a farming boom – to the Midlands and north-west. Bankers such as Barnard brothers of Bedford, the Gurneys of Norwich and neighbouring regional towns, Vincent Stuckey of Somerton (near Taunton), in the early nineteenth century had a rising tide of deposits for which they sought profitable, secure, short-term outlets – and these they found overwhelmingly in the discount market, taking portfolios of bills from bankers in commercial and industrial areas, where the demands for credit were greater than locally available supplies. Agriculture was financing trade in the main rather than long-term investment and perhaps this remained a largely seasonal trade, from after the harvest to the spring.

Farmers often needed credit themselves in the months before harvest. But the flows were nonetheless important. They certainly did not dry up at the time of maximum expansion of agriculture in the long wars – rather the reverse. This period was just when they were becoming institutionalized through the bill brokers, new financial intermediaries whose business developed rapidly after Thomas Richardson set up the first office in the City in 1800. Responses were being activated across the economy and institutional barriers between different sectors which might have blocked these stimuli were breaking down. Indeed new developments – national insurance companies, a national network of country bankers linked to London bankers and the bill brokers – show how, by the end of the eighteenth century, the forces mobilizing factors of production were being institutionalized.

Food supplies and agricultural prices

Industrialization meant the development of a non-agricultural labour force and, with this, a decline in the percentage of food producers in the occupied population and a consequent change in the structure of the labour force. In this way, discounting the external balance, the process of industrialization faces a constraint if agricultural productivity does not rise. Unless the declining proportion of the labour force left on the land produces more per head, to maintain total food supplies, prices will rise and cause a contraction of demand for the products of industry and a fall in the price of industrial goods – a 'scissors crisis', as it became known in Russia during the inter-war years. The labour aspect of this process can also be vital: assuming a stable population, labour for the rising non-agricultural activities has to come from the agricultural sector. With much labour in agriculture underemployed, with a very low (or zero) marginal product, such purging of the labour force on the farms can come without significant loss of output even if the productivity of those more fully employed does not rise. Further, in a context of rising population, total production in agriculture has to rise, as well as productivity. This will make extra investment demands on agriculture to achieve an increase in total production, but will ease the problems of the labour force in industry. The context of a stable population will ease the problem of total investment in agriculture, but may raise problems of getting labour transfers to industry.

Then comes the problem of the external balance – the balance of payments constraints which may be imposed by the failure of agricultural productivity and output to rise in step with other sectors. In twentieth-century India, for example, agriculture has been a key foreign exchange earner, in primary commodities like rice, wheat, leather, jute and tea. If the balance between population, growth, internal demand for food and agricultural output becomes adverse, food imports have to be at the expense of other imports needed for industrialization, whether raw materials, capital equipment or services. Foreign loans also have to be serviced from export earnings. Rising population, by causing more land to be mortgaged to growing food crops unless agricultural productivity and output increase, will lead to the reduction of 'raw material' agricultural crops and exports, thus reducing the export of primary products (and foreign exchange earnings from them) even if no food imports are required.

In the case of eighteenth and early nineteenth century Britain this potential external constraint was not nearly so relevant, and agriculture did not have the same importance as a foreign exchange earner. Indeed, some relationships were reversed. In the first place the international context was very different. Growth industries in Britain in the late eighteenth century were export orientated, earning their own foreign exchange for imports. Raw cotton imports were less than one third the value of cotton exports; iron exports were always higher than imports of bar iron. The context also favoured the export of manufactured goods, no longer the case for twentieth-century underdeveloped countries. By the last quarter of the century the level of world costs set by handicraft methods were beginning to be undercut by mechanization in Britain, particularly in cotton spinning and in the production of iron. During the first half of the nineteenth century protectionism was at a low ebb abroad, with agricultural interests politically dominant in many countries. Formal and informal empire gave open access to many foreign markets. Indeed the present-day logic was reversed in large measure. In certain markets British exports were argued to be dependent variables upon imports from primary produce suppliers elsewhere in the world, who lacked the necessary sterling credits for buying from Britain in the absence of their sales to Britain, which, because of the nature of their economies, had to be initially in primary produce. Less strain also fell upon the balance of payments on the import side. After 1780, little foreign capital earned dividends from Britain – indeed the net flow of interest and dividends was inward – and there were no heavy imports of capital equipment or services.

The sources of expansion of agriculture output are several. The most prominent for the eighteenth century were inputs of more land and more labour, with the capital required to bring it into production. Greater efficiency also came to the use of land and the deployment of labour, which would require better management to become effective. Larger farms with improved organization, where the labour force might be able to work more days per year and where other economies of scale in equipment, draught animals, and the handling of crops and stock could be realized, were further sources of higher productivity. Technical change and innovation were integral with such developments. New rotations, new crops, better animals, improved equipment, could enhance the productivity of land (the value of output per acre) and the productivity of labour (output per man). Better drainage, transport and storage on the farm would also contribute. Specialist crops, such as hops, could greatly increase the value of output per acre and bring new possibilities of prosperity to small holdings and the family-worked farm.

Agricultural expansion and productivity were also encouraged by developments off the farm, in addition to the increase in demand, particularly urban demand. Improved transport to urban markets – by river, canal and road – was the most important of such measures reducing the cost of food in the towns and stimulating prices for the farmer at the same time. Such a fall in real costs of transport were potentially of benefit, to both the urban consumer and the farmer – but the effect of equalizing prices between town and country often led to an increase of farm prices in the countryside, which in difficult years produced hostility from countrymen in the destruction of turnpikes and the seizure of stocks held by merchants – the instruments and agents of the 'export' of local food supplies to distant markets.

One final point about agricultural productivity should be remembered. It is unreal to attempt such conceptual specification (let alone attempting to measure it) without the realization that no clear-cut frontiers existed between agriculture and other activities. In many regions rural industries expanded during the eighteenth century where labour was shared with farming. This was partly a question of an integrated family economy, with the work of man, wife and children contributing in different ways to the household's viability; partly it was a question of industrial work taking up the slack in the local need for agricultural labour – with seasonal underemployment, the over-supply of labour relative to the extent of land even at the peak of seasonal demands in plough time and harvest, and even the opportunity of working indoors on the loom on occasional days when the weather was simply too bad to be able to work in the fields. For these reasons, a poor record in agricultural productivity did not, by itself, necessarily imply an inefficient rural 'handicraft' economy.

Recent research (paradoxically, one might reflect, in historical demography more than agricultural history) has led to revisions in the estimates of the performance of British agriculture in the eighteenth century. When it was assumed that the national population was broadly static in the decades before 1740, estimates for the growth of output in agriculture (given other trends) were downgraded. Deane and Cole, for example, saw agricultural output in a rising trend, assessed at 0.24% p.a. for the period 1700–60, 0.47% p.a. in 1760–80, and 0.65% p.a. in 1780–1800. Professor Craft's new assessments, made for the earlier period in the light of the new assumption, following the research of Professor Wrigley and Dr Schofield, that population was rising at 0.16% p.a. in 1686–1730, and 0.46% in 1730–50, are that agricultural output grew by 0.60% p.a. 1700–60; 0.13% p.a. 1760–80, and by 0.75% p.a. in 1780–1800.[7]

Apart from the population assessments, what other trends lie behind these assertions (because they remain assertions in the absence of systematic recording of actual outputs)? A larger number of people were being fed by the output of British farms than had previously been n realized. At the same time an agricultural export surplus was rising between 1700 and 1750 as the domestic capacity of British agriculture expanded faster than domestic needs. A million quarters of grain (mainly wheat) were exported in the abundant harvest year of 1750 and nearly 400,000 quarters of wheat were flowing abroad annually throughout the 1740s, which represented almost a fifth of total British exports. Agricultural prices were falling in this period, in response to the expansion of output in advance of domestic demand – wheat from 40.2s. per quarter in 1710–14 to 26.8s. per quarter in 1740–44 (a fall in index numbers from 100 to 67). The price of a 4 lb. loaf in London fell from 5.7d. to 4.6d. in the same year. At the same time (largely because of falling food prices) real wages were rising. The effects of rising (or falling) real wages upon demand for food are complex – and impossible to quantify with great accuracy. Extra spending power is shared between food and drink, and other things (including the potential for extra leisure and savings). The lower a family's income, the higher the proportion of it which would be spent on basic foodstuffs, and the less elastic the choice in any further economies of expenditure on food. Beyond a critical threshold, with increased earnings a lower proportion of the increment will be spent on food compared with other things. A further complication results from changes in the price of food compared with non-food prices – elasticities of demand are also affected by such relative price movements as well as by changing incomes.

[7]   P. Deane and W. A. Cole, *British Economic Growth, 1660–1959* (London, 1967); N. F. R. Crafts, *British Economic Growth during the Industrial Revolution* (Oxford, 1985); E. A. Wrigley and R. Schofield, *The Population History of England, 1541–1871: A Reconstruction* (London, 1981). (See above p. 8.)

Opposite trends explain the re-assessment downwards of the rate of growth of agricultural output in the next period. Population was continuing to rise, and at a progressively faster rate. But real wages were stagnant, or declining on trend, at least in London and the agricultural South. Agricultural exports declined to the point at which Britain became a net importer after 1770 – although imports remained a tiny fraction of total consumption of cereals and only occurred in years when the domestic harvest was short. For example, in the very bad year of 1800 (the second bad harvest in succession) when stocks were exhausted, 1.3 million quarters of wheat were imported, just over 5 per cent of total consumption, which Sir John Sinclair reckoned could have required only 150,000 extra acres under cultivation. Agricultural prices increased on trend, and increased relative to other prices, with the population growth: wheat to 44.9*s.* per quarter in 1785–9 (112 in terms of the index based on 1710–14 as 100); and thence, under conditions of wartime relative scarcities, to 102.5*s.* per quarter (255) in 1810–14. London bread prices rose to 6.1*d.* for the 4 lb. loaf in 1705–9 and 14.6*d.* in 1810–14.

Such trends in agricultural exports, real wages, and prices were less favourable for maintaining the growth of demand for agricultural output in the second half of the eighteenth century, but qualifications have to be made. Wage rates increased in the Midlands and the industrial and mining areas of the north in the 1760s and 1780s, so that the growth of effective demand may well have been underestimated, particularly as population was growing more rapidly in these regions than in the south. Too much stress may have been placed upon bread and wheat in these arguments; much of the cereal crop went into drink rather than bread and there are great unknowns as far as the consumption trends of meat are concerned. A great increase in the sheep population took place in the eighteenth century, and in much of the new farming practices which characterized progressive agriculture in the 'Norfolk' rotations and 'convertible' husbandry, the growth in animal numbers was integral with the extension of straw crops (animal dung being the essential source of fertility on the farm). The suggested numbers of cattle, on the other hand, scarcely kept up with population growth. Little can be said with certainty. Market records, particularly the Smithfield numbers, are notoriously misleading. Average weights of beasts coming to market were said to have risen by a quarter over the century and cattle came to maturity earlier, so a greater rate of turnover was possible within the slowly rising total stock. But even so the lag in numbers is significant. Of the numbers of pigs, which were probably the greatest source of meat for the poor, nothing can be said; while trends in the consumption of eggs, poultry, not to mention wild rabbits, pigeons and their like, remain unquantifiable mysteries.

From the farmer's and landlord's point of view rising prices gave a continuing stimulus for further enclosure and rising output, clearly demonstrated by the extraordinary assault on waste lands and poor upland soils to grow corn during the near-famine years of the long wars. Net corn output may have been growing at 7 per cent per decade in the 1780s, rising to double that rate in wartime (probably at the expense of non-corn output). These special problems of the 1790s and the first decade of the new century were not just the further projection of the peacetime trends since the mid-century, but were seen to validate the pessimism of Malthus and his contemporaries about the balance between food supplies and population. However, in retrospect one can see the great responsiveness of British agriculture to the very high wartime prices, which produced such an increase in demand that (for farmers and landlords) an opposite crisis of low agricultural prices, low rents and a fall in the price of land dominated the rural scene for the next twenty years of peace.

Agricultural practices and internal demand

Fluctuations in agricultural prices in the short-term, dependent upon the bounty of individual harvests, and on trend, generate 'income effects' which influence the economy as a whole, no less than the trends in demand for food affect progress in agriculture. The essential point is whether, with a fall in food prices such as occurred in 1720–50, the fall in income and spending of the farm sector was compensated (either more or less) by an increase in demand for non-food products by the consumers of food, whose incomes were not affected by its production. The opposite position then has to be argued for the second half of the century: did the increase in income and spending of the farm sector compensate for any fall in demand occasioned for non-food producers by rising food prices? Both sides can gain if the fall in food prices comes from a fall in the real costs of production on the farm or from a fall in the real costs of transport and distribution, closing the margin between prices at the farm gate and in the shops. Then lower prices are good for the food buyer, enabling more non-food buying potentially[8] from the same wages, and not detrimental to the demand generated by farmers and distributors, whose lower costs have accommodated the fall in price.

The number of food buyers in the country (which included the majority of families even in rural society, which had at their head a farm

[8]   The extra potential margin of purchasing power generated by a fall in food prices might also be shared with buying more food, working less or saving more.

labourer working for money wages) outnumbered by many times those receiving extra income from higher food prices. These benefits would be confined to farmers in the first instance, whose profits would be enhanced, and eventually the landlords, if higher farm prices continued long enough to work through into higher rents, as leases were renegotiated. Moreover the extra incomes of farmers and landlords were not likely to be as stimulating for the demand for basic industrial products as income in the wider structure of demand from the food buyers. Farmers and landlords would probably have had a higher propensity to save, in the first place, and would probably then have spent relatively more on services, improvements in housing and the like. When the working masses spent a higher proportion of money wages on food, they had to economize on buying clothes and household goods; when farmers became richer there was always talk of new pianos and dancing masters for their wives and daughters.

Even at the beginning of the eighteenth century, when up to four-fifths of the population lived in a rural setting and agriculture directly employed possibly half the working population, the three-deck structure of English rural society – landlord, tenant farmer, farm labourer – strongly influenced the demand effects of movements in agricultural prices – which would have been very different in a 'peasant' society, where the purchasing power of most families would have varied directly, rather than inversely, with the price of food. There is also the fact that the fall in food prices between 1714 and 1750 was occasioned by increased supply, which itself would have generated more employment on the land and in the 'downstream' processing industries. As the balance between the number of farmers and the food consumers changed over the century, with the changing economic structure, urbanization and the further proletarianization of rural society, so the income effects of changing food prices would have become more prominent.

Food prices were now on a rising trend. However, these direct income effects have to be set against the steady increase in the rate of population growth, and the fact that wage rates almost doubled in the industrializing regions and the volume of employment (the number of days per year in work) probably also increased in the non-agricultural sector. At all events it is doubtful whether industrial growth was adversely affected by rising food prices until the wartime scarcities of the 1790s – and this was in a context where the internal market was several times the extent of exports, even if industrial exports began to grow relatively faster than total production after 1780. The level of demand of food consumers (including the farm labourers) was collectively more important than the level of demand of farmers and landowners for basic industrial consumer goods.

The farm market itself seems not to have been critically important for the iron industry, by way of demand for implements – nationally if not regionally. The changes in these economic flows were more important on the savings side where, as we have seen, the surpluses of landowners and farmers were being mobilized by the last quarter of the century through the country bankers, and also fertilizing investment in transport, mining and the growth of towns. Demand constraints did develop during the war years, even though agricultural labourers' money wage rates seem to have kept pace on trend with the rising costs of living.

Recent studies (not cited in footnotes)

Agricultural change

R. C. Allen, 'The growth of labour productivity in early modern English agriculture', *Explorations in Economic History* XXV (1988); J. D. Chambers and G. E. Mingay, *The Agricultural Revolution* (London, 1966); M. Havinden, 'Agricultural progress in open-field Oxfordshire', *Agricultural History Review* IX (1961); R. V. Jackson, 'The growth and deceleration of English agriculture, 1660–1770', *Economic History Review* XXXVIII (1985); M. Overton, 'Estimating crop yields from … East Anglia, 1585–1735', *Journal of Economic History* XXXIX (1979); M. Turner, *Enclosures in Britain, 1770–1830*' (London, 1984).

Agriculture and industrialization

E. Boserup, *The Conditions of Agricultural Growth* (London, 1965); C. W. Chalkin and J. R. Wordie, *Town and Countryside, 1660–1860* (London, 1989; E. L. Jones (ed.), *Agriculture and Economic Growth in England, 1650–1815* (London, 1967); *Agriculture and the Industrial Revolution* (Oxford, 1974); P. K. O'Brien, 'Agriculture and the Industrial Revolution…', *Economic History Review* XXX (1977); 'Agriculture and the home market for English industry, 1660–1820', *English Historical Review* (1985); E. M. Ojala, *Agriculture and Economic Growth* (London, 1965); J. T. Ward and R. G. Wilson (eds), *Land and Industry* (Newton Abbot, 1971).

7

Population Growth and Economic Change in the Eighteenth and Nineteenth Centuries

Robert Woods

All would agree that there existed a reciprocal relationship between population growth and economic change in eighteenth-century England. Population growth encouraged economic expansion and the latter in its turn facilitated the former, but which was the chicken and which the egg? Is it possible that the modern rise of population was initiated by forces largely unrelated to those economic conditions prevailing in the early eighteenth century; that demography was then independent of economics, but became dependent in the nineteenth century, when industrialization and urbanization together created a new society? Might the economic transformation known as the industrial revolution have required as one of its pre-conditions the prior control of population growth, so that per capita incomes could rise well beyond the level necessary for subsistence?

These are large and important questions which are fundamental to an understanding of Britain's economic and demographic history.[1]

[1]   The following represent some of the most important references on population and economic development in Britain in the eighteenth and nineteenth centuries: P. Deane and W. A. Cole, *British Economic Growth, 1688–1959* (Cambridge, 1967, 2nd edn); H. J. Habakkuk, *Population Growth and Economic Development since 1750* (Leicester, 1972); J. D. Chambers, *Population, Economy and Society in Pre-Industrial England* (Oxford, 1972); R. D. Lee and R. S. Schofield, 'British population in the eighteenth century', in: R. Floud and D. McCloskey (eds), *The Economic History of Britain since 1700, Volume 1. 1700–1860* (Cambridge, 1981), pp. 17–35.

However, they are far from easy to answer. First, we lack reliable and comprehensive data upon which to base the sophisticated analyses required to resolve these outstanding issues. This is not to say that historians are working in complete ignorance, but their bricks are often made without straw and their quantitative series are tantalizing in their appearance of reliability. Secondly, the models necessary to give shape to the economic–demographic relationships are not yet particularly well developed. The most simple stress the interplay between population and resources; others talk of phases, cycles and chance occurrences affecting a number of time series which are interlinked; while a third group of models emphasizes the emergence of an increasingly spatially differentiated economy, in which advanced urban industrial regions feed on the surplus population drawn from the rural periphery. All of these models are in some sense partial, none is amenable to formal testing, but as always certain interpretations, which may differ from one to another only in matters of emphasis, will appear most plausible to members of a particular generation of historians. Despite the simplicity of the models available, it is lack of evidence which limits our understanding.

This chapter offers some discussion of these issues from the standpoint of the demographer, rather than the economic historian. It is divided into three principal sections. The first considers the theoretical arguments that should apply to the causes and consequences of rapid population growth in an economy and society like eighteenth and nineteenth-century Britain. The second section deals with the empirical evidence as it relates to the changing size and structure of the population, together with the mortality, fertility and migration components. The final section summarizes the state of knowledge as it exists in the late 1980s and outlines a number of unresolved problems.

The arguments

Expectations about the economic structure of a pre-industrial society may be arranged under four headings, as follows:

Population and food

It would be expected that the price of food should be positively related to the rate of population growth; once the latter begins to increase for some reason the former will also be raised. The price of food will of course be influenced by other factors, especially in the short term, but the long-term influence of population growth rates will characterize the economy. Since the level of real wages is inversely related to food prices, real wage rates will also be inversely connected with the rate of population growth. Here we may have the central tie that binds food, wages and population together in all pre-industrial societies. Even those that are not heavily monetized, as Britain was in 1700, will find that access to food is restricted as the rate of population growth accelerates.[2]

However, it is also likely that food production itself will be limited by a mechanism that we now refer to as the law of diminishing returns. When technological advances in agriculture are slow or non-existent and all available land is already in use, then eventually the yield per unit of land will not repay ever increasing inputs of labour. In this argument old land may be more intensively cultivated up to a limiting point; new land could be brought into cultivation subject to the limitations of climate, soils and relief, and food could be imported from other regions or countries, but here again there are limitations set by the prevailing transport technology and the need to avoid political dependence.[3]

The rate of population growth must, by definition, be influenced in its turn by its three components: mortality, fertility and migration. It is easy to imagine how, in the most extreme case, if access to food is restricted then mortality will increase from starvation. Here the quantity of food available will act via mortality as a brake on the rate of population growth. Fertility will be affected by the age at which couples marry, the extent of permanent celibacy, the level of marital and illegitimate fertility. Again one can imagine circumstances in which in a pre-industrial society each one of these factors could be influenced by the prevailing conditions of material life. Marriages are postponed, fewer women marry, parents attempt to restrict their fertility and the unwed are more careful, all because life is harder or subject to disruption. Similarly, inter-regional, rural–urban or international migration may provide means of adjusting the rate of population growth in certain areas.

These points encompass the arguments developed by Thomas Robert Malthus in his essays on *The Principle of Population*. Malthus's ideas have always been controversial since their anti-utopian political emphasis

---

[2] There are many good discussions of these relationships, but one of the most straightforward is E. A. Wrigley, 'Malthus's model of a pre-industrial economy', in: J. Dupâquier and A. Fauve-Chamoux (eds), *Malthus Past and Present* (London, 1983), pp. 111–24. On the role of the population question in theories of economic growth see W. Eltis, *The Classical Theory of Economic Growth* (London, 1984).

[3] See E. Boserup, *Population and Technology* (Oxford, 1981); also R. D. Lee, 'Malthus and Boserup: a dynamic synthesis', in: D. Coleman and R. Schofield (eds), *The State of Population Theory* (Oxford, 1986), pp. 96–130.

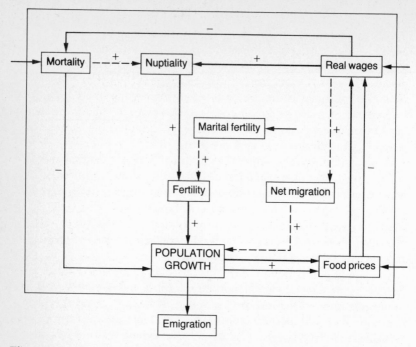

Figure 1 A systems model of the relationships between population and economy in a pre-industrial society

makes them a necessary target for social revolutionaries, yet in recent years his contributions as an economist and particularly as an historian of the eighteenth century have come to be appreciated more fully. Since Malthus was a subtle thinker who shifted ground not insubstantially between his first *Essay* and subsequent writings his work requires careful examination, but is at the same time open to caricature.[4] Figure 1 captures the points that are of most relevance for economic historians and demographers.[5] It shows a system in balance, where the rate of population growth is checked if for some reason it gets out of step with food

[4]   D. Winch, *Malthus* (Oxford, 1987) provides a readable and recent introduction. E. A. Wrigley, 'Elegance and experience: Malthus at the Bar of History', in: D. Coleman and R. Schofield (eds), *The State of Population Theory* (Oxford, 1986), pp. 46–64 considers Malthus the historian.

[5]   See R. S. Schofield, 'The relationship between demographic structure and environment in pre-industrial Western Europe', in: W. Conze (ed.), *Sozialgeschichte de Familie in der Neuzeit Europas* (Stuttgart, 1976), pp. 147–60; E. A. Wrigley and R. S. Schofield, *The Population History of England, 1541–1871: A Reconstruction* (London, 1981), especially ch. 11.

production. It is a homeostatic system dominated by negative feedback. The outer circuit (shown by thin, continuous lines in figure 1) represents Malthus's positive check, the central mechanism described in his essay of 1798. It works in the following way: any increase in the rate of population growth will push up the price of food, which will reduce the level of real wages, which if severe or general enough will increase the level of mortality, which ultimately will serve to reduce the rate of population growth. In this sequence death draws the balance with starvation and famine as its agents.

In his second *Essay* of 1803 and subsequent editions, Malthus suggested another means by which the rate of population growth could be checked. This preventive check is shown as the inner circuit in figure 1 (thick continuous lines). Now an increse in the rate of population growth would, by reducing the level of real wages, prompt those intending to get married to postpone their plans, that is it would increase the mean age at first marriage and perhaps also raise the level of permanent female celibacy. Either way lower levels of nuptiality would reduce the overall fertility rate and hence the rate of population growth. For Malthus this preventive check represented a way in which human behaviour could be changed via the practice of moral restraint, so that the misery and vice associated with the positive check could be avoided.

Although the arguments outlined above, particularly those linking population, food supplies and wages and the form of the mortality-led positive check, are general, the nuptiality-led preventive check described by Malthus not only requires society to be structured in a particular way in order for it to be effective, but it also makes the claim that such a structure has significant demographic, and thus perhaps economic, advantages. The preventive check will be most effective in those societies where marriage, the establishment of an independent household and the commencement of sexual intercourse (at least for the wife) all take place at the same time. In such societies illegitimate fertility will be low (although bridal pregnancy may be common) and a couple will have to have sufficient means to set up a new household, normally in a dwelling separate from both sets of parents, before the marriage can take place. By these means the marriage rate will respond to prevailing economic circumstances, and rates of population and economic growth will be kept in line.[6]

---

[6]   See J. Haynal, 'European marriage patterns in perspective', in: D. V. Glass and D. E. C. Eversley (eds), *Population in History* (London, 1965), pp. 101–43; and 'Two kinds of pre-industrial household formation system', in: R. Wall, J. Robin and P. Laslett (eds), *Family Forms in Historic Europe* (Cambridge, 1983), pp. 65–104.

However, it is possible to imagine three additional relationships which lie on or entirely outside the borders of the Malthusian scheme (shown by dashed lines in figure 1). In a predominantly agrarian society largely composed of small farmers, virtually the only means open to a couple of becoming financially independent of their parents is to gain access to land, for a son to inherit from his father. If mortality were to increase, opportunities to inherit would also increase and nuptiality would respond positively to mortality. But where large landowners employ agricultural labourers, or the non-agricultural proportion of the population is high, such an association would be weak even where the rules for family formation are unchanged. In a highly mobile society with an active market for agricultural land and a substantial urban sector, one would also expect to find that net migration had an influence on the rate of growth of a region's population. Such an association would act as an additional link between real wages and the rate of population growth. The third and final relationship, and the one outside Malthus's scheme, is concerned with marital fertility. For Malthus the deliberate restriction of fertility within marriage could not be countenanced, nor could abortion or infanticide, yet these are all far more direct and effective ways of limiting fertility. Their efficient practice could render the nuptiality-led preventive check redundant.

Finally, under this first heading it is worth noting at least one anti-Malthusian view on the relationship between agricultural production and the rate of population growth in a pre-industrial society. Ester Boserup has advanced the counter-argument that population pressure can promote increases in agricultural output and act as a general stimulus to development.[7]

The autonomous death rate

In Malthus's model of a pre-industrial economy mortality occupies an important place, but it is one tied closely to the state of the economy and especially the price of food. However, a number of economic and demographic historians have argued that violent short-run fluctuations in the death rates of such societies were more likely to have been caused by epidemics than food shortages and that as such they were independent of the economy's level of development and its rate of population growth.[8] Returning to figure 1, let us suppose that the arrow entering the mortality

[7]   Boserup, *Population and Technology*; see also D. B. Grigg, *Population Growth and Agrarian Change* (Cambridge, 1980).
[8]   See Chambers, *Population, Economy and Society*; M. W. Flinn, *The European Demographic System, 1500–1820* (Brighton, 1981).

box from the left represents a short series of substantial epidemics of bubonic plague, smallpox or 'the sweat', for example. How will the system respond? One possibility is that fertility, via an increase in nuptiality, will increase, so replacing those that have been lost. Population will also decline, so reducing the price of food and increasing real wages, and so to nuptiality again. If the period subject to such epidemics were to be extended, then it is conceivable that generations would barely be able to replace themselves, despite lower food prices and higher real wages. Prolonged wars, especially when associated with epidemic mortality, might have the same effect.

The autonomous death rate concept can be made complementary to the rest of the model shown in figure 1 by opening the formerly closed self-equilibrating system to external forces, whilst allowing the internal mechanism to persist. The negative link between real wages and mortality would not need to be removed, but it would be necessary to recognize that mortality could increase irrespective of the state of the economy. It is also important to point out that if disease patterns changed for any reason, including medical advances or administrative intervention, then mortality would fall, population growth would accelerate and the preventive check would be brought into play.

Small-scale commodity production

So far the arguments presented have been concerned exclusively with agrarian societies, however, such societies may also contain substantial numbers who are not directly engaged in agricultural production or who are only engaged on a part-time, perhaps a seasonal, basis. The traditional examples of such occupations are milling and blacksmithing, but if carting, brewing, baking, weaving, carpentry, building, shoemaking etc., were also to join the list, then the proportion of non-agricultural rural dwellers would be substantially increased. It might be argued, even within the framework of figure 1, that such developments would tend to foster the growth of population by allowing marriages to be contracted earlier and more people to marry since, for many, marriage does not now depend on the prior inheritance of land, but rather on the accumulation of non-agricultural wages.[9] One can also imagine how this small-scale

[9]   P. Kriedte et al., *Industrialization before Industrialization* (Cambridge, 1981); D. Levine, *Family Formation in an Age of Nascent Capitalism* (New York, 1977); and, 'Industrialization and the proletarian family in England', *Past and Present*, 107 (1985), pp. 168–203, provides a valuable illustration of these arguments for England, but see also D. C. Coleman, 'Proto-industrialization: a concept too many', *Econ. Hist. Review*, 36 (1983), pp. 435–48.

commodity production is likely to become concentrated in particular localities or certain regions, especially where resource endowments encourage that specialization. Combining these two points allows for regional differences in the rates of population growth and their positive association with non-agricultural employment opportunities. However, it should be the case that while the homeostatic system operates, the maximum rate of regional population growth will still be restrained by the population–food–wages mechanism and restrictions on nuptiality, but real wages may now be more closely atuned to the trade cycle than the price of food.

Urbanization

Despite being predominantly rural, many pre-industrial societies also possessed an elaborate urban network. Most of these urban places were administrative, ecclesiastical or market centres whose populations were supported by rural agricultural surpluses. If, as has been widely argued, the larger of these towns and cities acted as 'demographic sinks', that is they needed to absorb surplus rural populations to compensate for excessive mortality, then the proportion of any population living in such places would be likely to have an important effect on the rate of growth of the total population. For most pre-industrial societies this urban effect would be negligible, either because the level of urbanization was low or the towns themselves were small, but with larger towns, even one considerable metropolitan centre, the effect could be substantial. In this argument the effect on the rural population of rural to urban migration would be similar to that of permanent international emigration on the national population.[10]

These arguments about the economy and demography of pre-industrial societies can be summarized as follows. The essential mechanism links the rate of population growth and the price of food in the way depicted in figure 1. Disequilibrating forces will be counteracted by balancing mechanisms involving mortality or fertility. However, the system is not in perfect equilibrium; it may be influenced by essentially random attacks of epidemic disease and is thus not entirely closed. Disparities in rates of population growth may also exist not only between regions, but also between rural and urban environments. The former relates to the

[10]   J. de Vries, *European Urbanization, 1500–1800* (London, 1984) and E. A. Wrigley, *People, Cities and Wealth* (Oxford, 1987), especially part 2, contain disussions of these relationships.

development of by-employment or an entirely non-agricultural population, while the latter stems from the level of urbanization and, ultimately,
differentials in mortality rates. In this model, economy and demography
are interrelated, demography adjusts to economy but living standards are
in turn affected by the rate of population growth.

If the above represents a sketch of the relationships one would expect
to find in a pre-industrial society, how would economy and demography
be linked in a society that had been transformed by industrialization? The
conventional answer to this question dwells upon the notion of a
demographic transition in which high mortality and fertility rates are
replaced by low rates which reflect increasing control of mortality and
fertility. After a period of mismatch in which fertility greatly exceeds
mortality and population growth accelerates, the rate of growth declines
to the point of demographic stagnation. During the transition mortality is
principally affected by the combined influence of the agricultural,
industrial and sanitary revolutions, while urbanization and the increased
use of contraception ultimately serve to reduce marital fertility and
thereby replace the traditional preventive check. The old demographic
system if it survives at all does so in a form that is open to external
influence and is not internally self-regulating. Economic growth will now
be prompted by population expansion, although the association between
the two will become weaker over time. However, it is important to make
clear that industrialization alone may not be responsible for the new
demographic pattern. The formation of an urban industrial society also
involves social modernization to the extent that the links between
economic and demographic change may become blurred by radical and
coincidental changes in the way society is structured.[11]

The evidence

It is now high time for us to turn from arguments and speculations about
the demography and economy of pre- and post-industrial societies to
consider what is known about the relationships that existed in eighteenth-
and nineteenth-century Britain. However, before embarking on such a
task, it is important that we pause to review the nature of the data upon
which the exercise must rest.

The penultimate chapter of J. D. Chambers's *Population, Economy,
and Society in Pre-Industrial England* (footnote 1, above) was entitled

[11]   R. I. Woods, *Theoretical Population Geography* (London, 1982).

'Bricks without straw: the course of population change in the eighteenth century'. It is now over twenty years since the lectures on which the book was based were delivered. During this period there have been very considerable advances, particularly in the more ingenious use of old demographic sources. The first population census of Great Britain was not conducted until 1801; civil registration of births, marriages and deaths did not begin in England and Wales until 1837 and 1855 in Scotland. Any estimates of fertility and mortality prior to 1837 must be based, therefore, on the records of baptisms and burials in largely Anglican parish registers. Similarly, estimates of the size, composition and distribution of the population before 1801 will also need to be founded on aggregations from parish registers to which some inflation factor has been applied. This was the state of affairs to which Chambers referred, but since the publication of E. A. Wrigley and R. S. Schofield's *The Population History of England, 1541–1871: A Reconstruction* (footnote 5, above), in 1981, we now have available rather more bricks of a higher quality. Although the method of back projection employed by Wrigley and Schofield also uses Anglican parish registers the estimates of mortality, fertility and total population so derived are anchored to far more reliable evidence for the middle of the nineteenth century. Although their methods have attracted criticism, particularly with respect to the assumptions it is necessary to make in order to convert baptisms and burials into births and deaths, to allow for net migration and the consequences of having to use largely village registers, it is most likely that their results portray the most accurate picture of long-term demographic change in England that is likely to be attainable, given the sources available.[12] There remain problems in linking estimates derived from parish registers and those based on censuses and civil registration, but these are not insurmountable. It is also the case that relatively little is known about Scotland, Wales and the English regions compared with England as a single unit and about economic as opposed to demographic series.[13]

Despite these limitations on the quantity and reliability of the evidence now available, it is possible to sketch the essential elements of the changing demography of Britain.

[12]   See the contributions to R. I. Rotberg and T. K. Rabb (eds), *Population and Economy: From the Traditional to the Modern World* (Cambridge, 1986).
[13]   On Scotland, see M. Flinn (ed.), *Scottish Population History* (Cambridge, 1977). Neither Wales nor Monmouthshire is coverd by Wrigley and Schofield's estimates.

Total population

Table 1 shows the best available estimates of the changing population of England, Scotland, Wales and London. None of the figures is precise, although those based on censuses are more reliable than the others. The table illustrates several important properties of British population growth. First, late seventeenth-century stagnation was followed by slow growth, which only began to accelerate in the late eighteenth but especially the early nineteenth century. Secondly, England retained about 80 per cent of the British population. Thirdly, by the mid-seventeenth century London contained more people than Wales and by 1901 more people than Scotland. In 1601, 5 per cent of the English population lived in London; 11 per cent in 1801 and 15 per cent in 1901.

Mortality: the positive check and the autonomous death rate

Ideally, one would wish to have information about mortality categorized

Table 1 Population estimates in millions

	England	Scotland	Wales	Great Britain	London
1551	3.01				0.08
1601	4.11		0.35		0.20
1651	5.23		0.38		0.40
1701	5.06	1.04	0.39	6.49	0.58
1751	5.77	1.25	0.45	7.47	0.68
1801	8.66	1.63	0.59	10.88	0.96
1851	16.77	2.89	1.16	20.82	2.36
1901	30.52	4.47	2.01	37.00	4.54

Sources: England: 1551–1751, E. A. Wrigley and R. S. Schofield, *The Population History of England, 1541–1871* (London, 1981), table A3.1.
Scotland: 1701–1751, P. Deane and W. A. Cole, *British Economic Growth 1688–1959* (Cambridge, 1967), table 2.
Wales: 1601–1751, J. Williams (ed.), *Digest of Welsh Historical Statistics, Vol. 1* (Cardiff, 1985), p.6.
London: 1551–1751, E. A. Wrigley, *People, Cities and Wealth* (Oxford, 1987), table 7.3 and J. de Vries, *European Urbanization 1500–1800* (London, 1984), p. 270.
1801–1901: based on the Population Censuses of Great Britain.

by age, cause and geographical location, but this is only possible towards the end of the nineteenth century. For earlier periods there are estimates of the level of mortality, usually expressed in terms of life expectation at birth, and while it is possible to distinguish between crisis mortality and the normal level of background mortality, it may not prove easy to separate the various causes of crisis mortality. In its most pure form the Malthusian positive check should manifest itself as a subsistence crisis with famine a symptom of overpopulation. However, it is also likely that such subsistence crises will be combined with outbreaks of epidemic diseases; they may also coincide with military activity and trade depressions.[14]

The evidence presented by Wrigley and Schofield makes it quite clear that England did not suffer from repeated national subsistence crises in the period from the mid-sixteenth century.[15] There were of course periods of dearth, even regional crises, in the north west, but there were no significant national famines. There were epidemics of various forms, but their incidence was largely random in time and space apart from the emphasis on urban places, especially London. From Wrigley and Schofield's data it would appear that demographic crises had a relatively negligible impact on the course of long-term population change and thus, by implication, that the background level of mortality was of greater significance in determining the rate of population growth.[16] Table 2 gives estimates of life expectation at birth for England in 25-year periods. There are certainly fluctuations in e_0, ranging from low points in the fourth quarter of the seventeenth and the second quarter of the eighteenth centuries, to high points in the quarters surrounding 1600. From the middle of the nineteenth century e_0 begins a slow but continuous rise. Wrigley and Schofield have also provided estimates of infant mortality (q_0) by pooling the results of 13 family reconstitution studies drawn from rural parishes. These are also shown in table 2, together with an estimate of q_0 for England and Wales in the second half of the nineteenth century.

---

[14]   A. B. Appleby, *Famine in Tudor and Stuart England* (Liverpool, 1978), and J. D. Post, *The Last Great Subsistence Crisis in the Western World* (Baltimore, 1977), and *Food Shortage, Climatic Variability and Epidemic Disease in Preindustrial Europe: The Mortality Peak in the Early 1740s* (Ithaca, 1985), all present the case for subsistence crises, but Post's work does not relate well to Britain, and England especially.

[15]   Wrigley and Schofield, *Population History of England*, especially appendix 10.

[16]   S. Cotts Watkins and J. Menken, 'Famines in historical perspective', *Population and Development Review*, 11 (1985), pp. 647–75, argue that the long–term demographic impact of famines has, in any case, been overemphasized.

Table 2 Estimates of life expectation at birth (e_0) and infant mortality (q_0 per 1000 live births) for England

		e_0	q_0
1.	1551–75	35	
2.	1576–1600	39	
3.	1601–25	39	162
4.	1626–50	36	
5.	1651–75	35	170
6.	1676–1700	33	
7.	1701–25	36	195
8.	1726–50	33	
9.	1751–75	36	166
10.	1776–1800	37	
11.	1801–25	39	
12.	1826–50	40	149
13.	1851–75	41	154
14.	1876–1900	46	149
15.	1901–25	53	105
16.	1926–50	64	55
17.	1951–75	72	22

Sources: e_0 1551–1850: E. A. Wrigley and R. S. Schofield, *The Population History of England, 1541–1871* (London, 1981), table A3.1.

q_0 1601–1800: pooled data for 13 rural English parishes from E. A. Wrigley and R. S. Schofield, 'English population history from family reconstitution: summary results, 1600–1799', *Population Studies*, 37 (1983), p. 177.

e_0 and q_0 1851–1975: Registrar General's *Annual Reports* and *Decennial Reviews*.

As one would expect, higher levels of q_0 are associated with lower levels of e_0; both emphasize the apparently poor living conditions in the late seventeenth and early eighteenth centuries.

The central point to emerge from this discussion is that mortality remained relatively unchanged in the long-run despite sharp year-on-year fluctuations. In England, at least, it would be unwise to overstate the influence of crises, whether of the subsistence or epidemic variety, when compared with the background level of mortality. In Scotland, however, there is good evidence to suggest that there were repeated and severe crises in the seventeenth century at least and that the 1690s in particular was a period of famine in certain areas.[17] Elsewhere in Europe, wars plagues and famines also brought havoc, even in the eighteenth century, but in general subsistence crises became less frequent or were the result of warfare or the vicissitudes of climate in agriculturally marginal environments such as northern Europe. Like England, the Netherlands remained free from the positive check even in the seventeenth century.[18] Apart from the effects of war, it now seems likely that the influence of crisis mortality, whether of the form envisaged by Malthus or Chambers, was less important in the early-modern period in western Europe generally than has formerly been supposed.

If this is so, what factors were responsible for fluctuations in and ultimately the secular decline of the background level of mortality? Let us consider four possibilities. First, the cause of death patterns may change, but largely of their own accord. New diseases appeared, and old diseases became less active for reasons connected with the diseases themselves, rather than man's intervention or the state of economy and society. Secondly, medical knowledge and practice may develop, become more effective and more widely accessible. Thirdly, the standard of living of the population, especially in terms of its diet and housing, may improve, thereby reducing both morbidity and mortality. Fourthly, certain administrative advances, particularly in the fields of public health and sanitation, may affect mortality from the water-borne diseases.[19] There is some evidence for each of these possibilities, but little that is hard and fast until the late nineteenth and twentieth centuries. For example, it is likely that the port quarantine regulations developed in the seventeenth and eighteenth centuries helped to prevent the re-introduction of bubonic plague from the Middle East and that late eighteenth- and early nineteenth-century developments in smallpox vaccination helped to control that disease, but there are hardly any other examples of advances in public hygiene or medical care that could have had even a marginal effect on death rates until the late nineteenth century. It seems most likely that variations in the background level of mortality between regions and social groups were the consequence of vagaries in disease patterns, the nature of

[17]   See Flinn, *Scottish Population History*, for details of the Scottish experience.
[18]   O. Turpeinen, 'Fertility and mortality in Finland since 1750', *Population Studies*, 33 (1979), pp. 101–14 and J. A. Faber, 'Dearth and famine in pre-industrial Netherlands', *Low Countries Yearbook*, 13 (1980), pp. 51–64 provide interesting and contrasting examples.
[19]   T. McKeown, *The Modern Rise of Population* (London, 1976), outlines these possibilities and R. I. Woods and J. H. Woodward (eds), *Urban Disease and Mortality in Nineteenth-Century England* (London, 1984), offer a critique.

the environment and the standard of living of the inhabitants. Scottish crofters and Kentish yeomen probably experienced different life chances, but these changed only slowly and not always for the better until significant advances were made in public health and medical science.[20]

A further issue that affects attempts to generalize about background, as opposed to crisis, mortality is the importance of deaths in infancy and early childhood. When life expectation at birth is low (30–35), as many as a quarter of all those dying will be infants. It is therefore quite possible that variations in life expectation over time and through space will be critically affected by infant mortality rates. By European standards, infant mortality in England was towards the low side of the range, largely because the practice of mothers breastfeeding their infants was almost universal. Where wet-nurses were used or babies were not breastfed at all, infant mortality of at least 300 per 1,000 live births would be expected, twice the English rate. It is possible that fluctuations in the national infant mortality rate could have resulted from changes in the practice of breastfeeding or that the convergence of regional customs may also have affected the national rate. These are mere speculations, for very little is known about breastfeeding habits in Britain before the twentieth century, but what is known about infant mortality rates suggests a relatively uniform pattern of breastfeeding.[21]

Fertility: the preventive check and the control of marital fertility

Once again, thanks to Wrigley and Schofield's book, we are able to chart the changing pattern of fertility over the period since the mid-sixteenth century.[22] Their estimates of the gross reproduction rate (GRR – the number of female children a woman might expect to have borne by the end of her reproductive period) are shown in table 3, together with supplementary data for the nineteenth and twentieth centuries. Fertility reached a peak in the first quarter of the nineteenth century (11) and thereafter it declined to the 1930s (16). Fertility was also high in the late sixteenth century (1, 2), but it fell to reach a low point in the late seventeenth century, followed by a steady rise in the eighteenth century.

[20]   F. B. Smith, *The People's Health, 1830–1910* (London, 1979), gives a very useful overview of Victorian conditions.
[21]   R. I. Woods, P. A. Watterson and J. H. Woodward, 'The causes of the rapid decline of infant mortality in England and Wales 1861–1921. Parts I and II', *Pop. Studies*, 42 (1988), pp. 343–66, and 43 (1989), pp. 113–32.
[22]   This section relies heavily on Wrigley and Schofield, *Population History of England*, and C. Wilson and R. I. Woods, 'Fertility in England: a long-term perspective' (unpublished paper, 1988).

Table 3 Estimates of the gross reproduction rate (GRR), the indexes of overall fertility (I_f) marital fertility (I_g) non-marital fertility (I_h) and nuptiality(I_m), the crude birth rate (CBR) and crude death rate (CDR)

	GRR	I_f	I_g	I_h	I_m	CBR	CDR
1. 1551–75	2.41	0.344	0.654	0.015	0.520	34.94	28.42
2. 1576–1600	2.29	0.335	0.653	0.018	0.499	33.22	24.22
3. 1601–25	2.25	0.324	0.654	0.018	0.481	32.72	24.82
4. 1626–50	2.11	0.309	0.648	0.012	0.464	31.46	26.22
5. 1651–75	1.91	0.271	0.643	0.006	0.416	28.58	28.36
6. 1676–1700	2.07	0.310	0.640	0.009	0.476	31.22	30.28
7. 1701–25	2.23	0.326	0.634	0.013	0.504	31.74	27.86
8. 1726–50	2.25	0.333	0.633	0.018	0.513	33.74	30.50
9. 1751–75	2.38	0.346	0.650	0.026	0.501	34.24	27.26
10. 1776–1800	2.64	0.387	0.666	0.042	0.552	35.56	26.46
11. 1801–25	2.91	0.421	0.668	0.054	0.598	40.18	25.38
12. 1826–50	2.57	0.364	0.669	0.041	0.514	36.04	22.54
13. 1851–75	2.49	0.359	0.670	0.045	0.502	35.82	22.22
14. 1876–1900	2.07	0.313	0.616	0.027	0.484	32.28	19.26
15. 1901–25	1.42	0.233	0.465	0.019	0.481	24.02	14.26
16. 1926–50	0.95	0.174	0.334	0.016	0.496	16.16	12.24
17. 1951–75	1.15	0.188	0.250	0.050	0.690	16.76	11.72

Sources: GRR, CBR and CDR, 1551–1850: E. A. Wrigley and R. S. Schofield, *The Population History of England, 1541–1871* (London, 1981), table A3.1.

I_f, I_g, I_h and I_m: estimates from C. Wilson and R. I. Woods, 'Fertility in England: A long-term perspective (unpublished paper, 1988).

GRR, CBR and CDR, 1851–1975: Registrar General's *Annual Reports* and *Decennial Reviews*.

Given the availability of mortality and fertility series it is possible to judge the contribution of both to the rate of population growth. This task was originally performed by Wrigley and Schofield themselves and is repeated here using the 17 25-year averages for e_0 and GRR given in tables 2 and 3. Figure 2 shows the result of plotting fertility (GRR) against mortality (e_0) on axes that have been constructed to allow the rate of natural growth to be read off the parallel, diagonal lines. Before the nineteenth century (point 11) the natural growth rate of England's population was affected by movement in both the vertical and horizontal axes, but in the eighteenth century growth rates were particularly

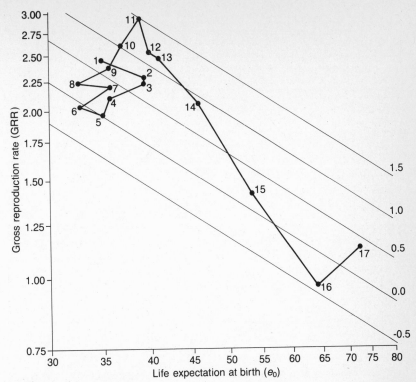

Figure 2 The relationship between fertility (GRR) and mortality (e_0) England, 1551–1975 (see tables 2 and 3)

associated with changes in fertility rather than mortality. This is one of the central findings of Wrigley and Schofield's work. From the late nineteenth century (14) mortality and fertility both declined rapidly and continuously.

Why did fertility rise and fall? Were its fluctuations tied to the economy via nuptiality in the way envisaged in figure 1? These are important questions that may only be answered by disaggregating the components of fertility trends. Marital and non-marital fertility must be separated and the effects of age at marriage and proportions marrying on nuptiality distinguished. Table 3 goes some way to tackling this issue by presenting the four fertility indices originally devised by the Princeton demographer, Ansley J. Coale.[23] The index of overall fertility (I_f) is

[23]   The construction of these indices is discussed at length in A. J. Coale and S. Cotts Watkins (eds), *The Decline of Fertility in Europe* (Princeton, 1986).

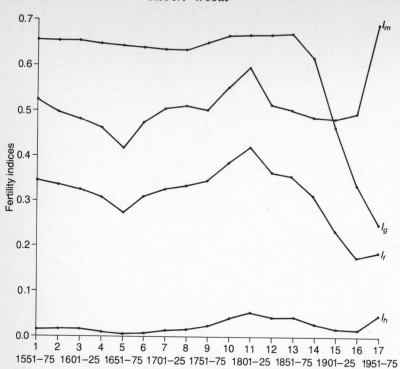

Figure 3 Trends in fertility indices England, 1551–1975 (see table 3)

influenced by the level of marital fertility (I_g), non-marital or illegitimate fertility (I_h) and the index of proportion married or the level of nuptiality (I_m). If illegitimate fertility is negligible, then overall fertility will be approximated by the product of marital fertility and the proportion married ($I_f = I_g . I_m$ if $I_h = 0$). A further property of these indices is that they are indirectly standardized on an age-specific marital fertility schedule that captures a pattern of largely biologically determined human fertility. When I_g is high (over 0.6, for example) there is good reason to suppose that members of the population concerned are not attempting to limit their marital fertility artificially, in order to meet some particular ideal family size. Demographers often describe the resulting pattern as natural fertility.

The four fertility indices are plotted in figure 3. They give clear evidence of the important contribution made by long-run changes in I_m to the level of fertility (I_f). Although marital fertility was not exactly constant there was very little change until the last half of the nineteenth

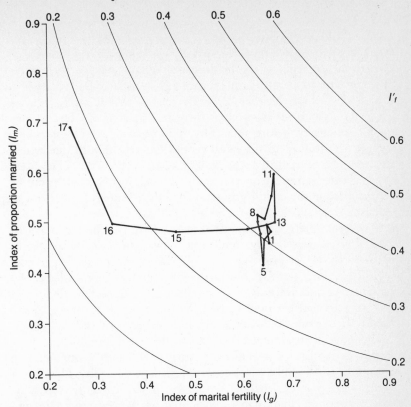

Figure 4 The index of proportion married (I_m) and the index of marital fertility (I_g), England, 1551–1975 (I_f is shown on the isolines, see table 3 and figure 3)

century when I_g fell below 0.6 for the first time.[24] Compared with the influence of I_m or I_f the effect of non-marital fertility was indeed negligible. If we assume, as we know would be reasonable, that I_h is very low then I_m may be plotted against I_g in the fashion of figure 4. The curved isolines trace equal values of I'_f, that is an approximation of I_f. Figure 4 merely helps to reinforce the point that until the third quarter of the nineteenth century any changes that occurred in fertility were almost entirely determined by nuptiality, but since that time fertility has been limited within marriage.[25]

[24]   C. Wilson, 'Natural fertility in pre-industrial England', *Population Studies*, 38 (1984), pp. 225–40.
[25]   R. I. Woods, 'Approaches to the fertility transition in Victorian England', *Pop. Studies*, 41 (1987), pp. 283–311.

Despite the very clear pictures provided by figures 3 and 4 it is most important, from the point of view of interpretation, that the components of nuptiality should also be distinguished. The index I_m, for example, is subject to the influence of age at marriage among females as well as the proportion who are permanently celibate. It is unusual to find societies in which these two variables are positively related. Where marriage takes place in the teens or early twenties there will be relatively few women who do not marry before their fiftieth birthday. Conversely, where marriages are delayed to the late twenties or early thirties one would expect to find a substantial proportion of women who never get married. These two cases represent the extremes, although many examples can be found for both in the middle ground, where the relationship need not be so precise.

It now seems likely that in England overall fertility, whether measured by GRR or I_f, was largely influenced by variations in the extent of permanent female celibacy up until the beginning of the eighteenth century, but during the eighteenth century it was more affected by changes in the mean age at marriage. This is an important finding. It means, as Schofield has pointed out, that 'what needs to be explained, therefore, is not only the change in emphasis from celibacy to age-at-marriage movements around 1700, but also the fact that changes in age at marriage in the late eighteenth and early nineteenth centuries were unusually large.'[26] Whilst it is clear what needs to be explained, it is not obvious what that explanation should be. There certainly was a tie between economic circumstances, measured by the real wage rate, and GRR, with nuptiality the intervening variable. But the association was both lagged and inexact. It seems likely that real wages affected economic opportunities, which in turn influenced the ability to marry, especially in an agrarian society, but as we have already seen any form of transformation which shifts the economy towards the production of manufactured goods is likely to reduce the influence of farm inheritance by increasing the opportunity to earn higher wages away from the land.[27] It used to be thought that the process known as proto-industrialization could be held

[26] The quotation is taken from p. 15 of R. Schofield, 'English marriage patterns revisited', *Journal of Family History*, 10 (1985), pp. 2–20; see also D. R. Weir, 'Life under pressure: France and England, 1670–1870', *J. Econ. Hist.*, 44 (1984), pp. 27–47; and 'Rather never than late: celibacy and age at marriage in English cohort fertility, 1541–1871', *J. Family Hist.*, 9 (1984), pp. 341–55.

[27] Recent work by P. R. Galloway, 'Basic patterns in annual variations in fertility, nuptiality, mortality, and price in pre-industrial Europe', *Pop. Studies*, 42 (1988), pp. 275–303, stresses the unique position of England which, unlike the rest of pre-industrial Europe, escaped the positive check and had a population growth rate which was 'hardly affected by changes in prices'.

responsible for higher levels of nuptiality, but this relationship is now in some doubt. A more plausible argument would associate the reorganization of agriculture, which particularly affected the arable farming areas of eighteenth-century England and involved large numbers of farm servants becoming agricultural labourers, with the removal of restrictions on age at marriage by employers.[28]

As with nuptiality in the late eighteenth century, so with marital fertility in the late nineteenth; demographic data demonstrate their significance, but explanations are elusive. Fertility certainly did decline from the early decades of the nineteenth century, but after the 1870s marital fertility rather than nuptiality was the main contributor (I_g rather than I_m influenced I_f). Why did married couples begin to control their fertility? By what means was the control achieved? It is very likely that the answer to the first question does not involve factors which are particular to changes in the economy or the standard of living.[29] For most people, new and permissive social attitudes were of greater significance than the level of wages. Married couples began to plan their families by asking themselves how many children they should have, and then making efforts to implement that plan. These important social changes suggest radical shifts in the status of women and their ability to bargain with their husbands over matters of intercourse, child rearing and their employment outside the home. It is still, and will probably always remain, unclear by what means family limitation was practised. The most likely methods are withdrawal and sexual abstinence, but it is possible that induced abortion also played a role in reducing the number of pregnancies that went to full term. New appliance methods of contraception did become more widely available just before and increasingly after the First World War, but in the last decades of the nineteenth century only traditional and often ineffective methods could be used.

The preventive check was still in operation in the late nineteenth and early twentieth centuries. If anything it became more effective in these decades than it had been in the previous half century and has remained so during the last 50 years, when mean age at marriage has fallen while divorce, remarriage and illegitimacy have increased.[30]

---

[28]   A. Kussmaul, *Servants in Husbandry in Early Modern England* (Cambridge, 1981).

[29]   See Woods, 'Approaches to the fertility transition in Victorian England'.

[30]   R. I. Woods and P. R. A. Hinde, 'Nuptiality and age at marriage in nineteenth-century England', *J. Family Hist.*, 10 (1985), pp. 119–44; R. I. Woods, 'What happened to the preventive check in late nineteenth-century England?' in: R. M. Smith (ed.), *Regional Population Patterns in the Past* (Oxford, forthcoming).

If one wished to oversimplify to an extreme degree, then the course of population change in England since 1600 would be characterized in the following way. Until the late nineteenth century national population growth rates were particularly influenced by changes in fertility, rather than mortality, and fertility was conditioned almost exclusively by the joint effects of the proportion of women remaining celibate and the mean age at first marriage.[31] The former was of most significance in the seventeenth century and the latter thereafter. From the late nineteenth century the decline of marital fertility became the most important influence on the rate of population growth, but its fall was also accompanied by the secular decline of mortality. Although the rate of population growth was not affected to any substantial degree by migration, the regional and rural–urban redistribution did have an important bearing on local rates.[32]

Urbanization, migration and the regional redistribution of population

It has never been easy to distinguish between urban and rural areas, but despite the problems there have been many attempts to define two mutually exclusive categories and to estimate the changing level of urbanization. Recently, E. A. Wrigley has taken this line of enquiry further by attempting to separate the agricultural from the non-agricultural within the rural population. His calculations are shown in table 4 and include Holland and France, as well as England. In each of the three countries there was a shift from rural to urban and out of agriculture. In Holland urbanization remained higher, but was stable, while in France it continued at a low level compared with England, where both urbanization and the rural non-agricultural sector moved on apace. The comparative figures in table 4 are interesting in their own right, but they also suggest differences in the level of agricultural productivity to the extent that over 60 per cent of England's population could be supported by the remainder at the end of the eighteenth century. Wrigley also suggests that one of England's remarkable features was the speed with which the population in the non-agricultural sector grew during the

[31] See the discussion in Wrigley, *People, Cities and Wealth*.
[32] What is known about internal and international migration is summarized in P. Clark and D. Souden (eds), *Migration and Society in Early Modern England* (London, 1987); A. Redford, *Labour Migration in England, 1800–1850* (Manchester, 1964); and D. Baines, *Migration in a Mature Economy: Emigration and Internal Migration in England and Wales, 1861–1900* (Cambridge, 1985).

Table 4 Percentage of population urban (U), rural agricultural (RA) ai rural non-agricultural (RNA), England, Holland and France, 1500–1800

	England			Holland			France		
	U	*RA*	*RNA*	*U*	*RA*	*RNA*	*U*	*RA*	*RNA*
1500							9.1	72.7	18.2
1520	5.5	76.0	18.5						
1550				20.8	59.6	19.6			
1600	8.0	70.0	22.0	29.0	50.0	21.0	8.7	68.9	22.3
1650				37.1	41.6	21.3			
1670	13.5	60.5	26.0						
1700	17.0	55.0	28.0	38.9	40.3	20.8	10.9	63.3	25.8
1750	21.0	46.0	33.0	35.1	42.9	22.1	10.3	61.4	28.2
1800	27.5	36.3	36.3	38.6	44.3	22.6	11.1	58.7	30.2

Source: E. A. Wrigley, *People, Cities and Wealth* (Oxford, 1987), tables 7.4, 7.8 and 7.9.

seventeenth and eighteenth centuries while, in comparison with other European countries, the growth of the agricultural population was far less remarkable.

Where did these urban and rural non-agricultural populations come from? The most obvious and traditional answer to this question is that the reorganization of agriculture in the seventeenth and eighteenth centuries meant the displacement of agricultural workers, who found new economic roles either in the towns, especially London, or in the expansion of commodity production in the countryside, with the handloom weavers and hosiery manufacturers providing perhaps the best examples. This argument about the inter-regional displacement of labour is now difficult to sustain in its simplest form. Consider figure 5 which shows the rates of natural increase and net migration for English counties in 1801–30. Two counties – Monmouthshire and Lancashire – have annual growth rates in excess of 2 per cent, but several others have rates between 1.5 and 2 per cent. Middlesex and Surrey, with the highest rates of net migration, fall into this category, but they also have the lowest rates of natural increase. Deane and Cole themselves make the following observation:

Hence when, as in Staffordshire and the West Riding, industry was widely diffused, it seems to have resulted in a rapid growth of population and little or no immigration from outside. But when, as in Lancashire and Warwick-

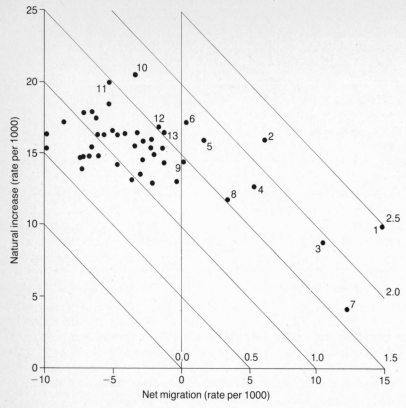

Figure 5 The relationship between rates of natural increase and net migration, English counties, 1801–1830

Key: 1 Monmouthshire; 2 Lancashire; 3 Surrey; 4 Cheshire; 5 W. Riding, Yorkshire; 6 Staffordshire; 7 Middlesex; 8 Warwickshire; 9 Durham; 10 Sussex; 11 Cornwall; 12 Nottinghamshire; 13 Cambridgeshire
Source: Phyllis Deane and W. A. Cole, *British Economic Growth 1688–1959* (Cambridge, 1967), table 26. Reproduced by kind permission.

shire, industrial development meant that a large proportion began to live in towns, we find that the county as a whole had a relatively small surplus of baptisms over burials, and it was compelled to draw heavily on the natural increase of its neighbours.[33]

Figure 5 does not entirely bear out this view, in the case of early nineteenth-century Lancashire at least, but it does confirm the point for

[33]   Deane and Cole, *British Economic Growth*, p. 121.

the London area. Most of what have become the major industrial counties were growing very substantially by natural increase, which was further supplemented by positive net migration rates.

The regional redistribution of population, and especially the rise of great urban centres, also had important consequences for national rates of population growth. One of the additional implications of figure 5 is that London almost certainly experienced particularly high levels of mortality when compared with the rest of Britain in 1800. Until the urban environment began to improve in the late nineteenth century, urbanization, and especially the increasing concentration of population in a small number of very large towns, would tend to counterbalance any improvements in mortality that may have occurred in rural areas.[34] This question of urban disamenities in terms of morbidity and mortality has to be set against the substantially higher wage rates that were available to urban workers in the northern industrial towns, as compared with the agricultural labourers of East Anglia or Wessex. Much has been made in recent years of this tension – health versus wages – but for many migrants it was not their own health that they were jeopardizing, rather the survival of successive generations of infants and young children lay at risk.[35] Eventually these urban health disamenities were removed, so that only differentials between social classes remain of great significance today, but the process of environmental improvement via public health was a long and slow business, which can only truly be seen to have taken effect with the decline of infant mortality from 1899. Before the twentieth century, increasing industrialization and the agglomeration economies that went with it encouraged urbanization and thereby probably helped to keep mortality at a high level and certainly retarded its substantial decline.[36]

Conclusion

Let us begin our assessment of what is now known, or thought to be known, by returning to figure 1. England certainly was a pre-industrial

[34]   See R. I. Woods and P. R. A. Hinde, 'Mortality in Victorian England: models and patterns', *Journal of Interdisciplinary History*, 18 (1987), pp. 27–54; and especially R. I. Woods, 'The effects of population redistribution on the level of mortality in nineteenth-century England and Wales' *J. Econ. Hist.*, 45 (1985), pp. 645–51.

[35]   J. G. Williamson, 'British mortality and the value of life, 1781–1931', *Pop. Studies*, 38 (1984), pp. 157–72.

[36]   Woods, Watterson and Woodward, 'Causes of the rapid decline of infant mortality'.

society in 1700, but it had at least two unusual features when compared with its European neighbours and many more when contrasted with oriental societies. First, the positive check, at least in its subsistence crisis form, does not seem to have been an important mechanism for demographic regulation in early modern England, but in Scotland and Ireland there were famines as there were in France and other parts of central and northern Europe. If death drew the balance, it did not do so via mass starvation. Secondly, although the study of migration is not well advanced in this period it is likely that Britain had a high level of geographical and occupational mobility. The estimates in table 4 bear witness to what must have been substantial rural–urban migration and transfer out of agriculture. They also attest to the increasing productivity of English agriculture. The preventive check was not peculiar to Britain, rather its influence covered much of north-western Europe. But in England the balancing mechanism via nuptiality appears to have been particularly effective as a means of adjusting to economic circumstances. Fluctuations in marital fertility were of no consequence at this time.

In short, the self-equilibrating system shown in figure 1, which has its origins in Malthus's *Essays*, not only describes the circumstances of seventeenth and eighteenth-century England (especially the inner circuit), but the mechanism itself worked rather well. What changed? At the end of the eighteenth century the positive link between food prices and the rate of population growth broke and with it the entire system ceased to be self-equilibrating. Population growth could accelerate without economic penalty. This was a singularly important event which, as has often been remarked, served almost to define the industrial revolution. In the nineteenth century population was able to grow, to become even more urbanized with ever diminishing numbers engaged in agricultural production, because of the productivity of home-based farming and the import of American and British colonial foodstuffs. When the rate of population growth was checked by the level of urban mortality, by local variations in nuptiality tied to disparities in age structure and occupational specialization, and ultimately by the decline of marital fertility, these checks were not directly tied to *changes* in food prices or real wages.

It seems most likely that a moderate rate of population growth, at about one per cent per annum, served to stimulate the market for consumer goods, building materials and passenger transport, thereby facilitating the upward spiral of economic growth and technological change. In the late twentieth century fertility and mortality are under control, below zero population growth and economic stagnation are more serious problems. The key turning points were as follows:

1590s	Last major regional subsistence crises in England (1690s in Scotland, 1840s in Ireland).
1700s	Mean age at first marriage became more important than permanent celibacy as an influence on nuptiality.
1800s	Peak rates of population growth and decay of association between growth rates and food prices.
1870s	Origin of the secular decline of marital fertility.
1899–1900	Start of the secular decline of infant mortality.

Many questions remain unresolved, as should be obvious from the above sketch. Apart from the difficulties of using historical demographic data, there are other issues which obscure our understanding. For example, above is given a short list of key turning points, each one of which has been identified in the empirical literature, although none has been explained entirely to the satisfaction of all economic and demographic historians. Again, much has been made of change over time in discussion of economic and demographic change to the extent that regional economies and demographies have been relatively ignored. There is some justification for this emphasis in southern England, which from an early stage became a single integrated regional economy dominated by London, but in the remainder of the British Isles segmented economies and localized labour markets were only slowly integrated into larger entities. However, when one reflects on the progress that has been made in the study of population, economy and society in the last twenty years, there is good reason to be optimistic that some of these issues will be more fully resolved before the turn of the century.

8

The Transformation of Work in European Industrialization

Kristine Bruland

Introduction

This chapter discusses relationships between technological change and the transformation of work in nineteenth-century Europe. The economic history of Europe since 1800 is essentially the history of industrialization, of structural change through which industrial sectors grew and non-agricultural activity came for the first time to dominate economic life. This structural change was associated, throughout Europe, with marked and sustained increases in growth rates of output and of productivity: the economic landscape of Europe was utterly changed. Technological innovation was central to this economic upheaval. The period as a whole saw radical and persistent technological changes in many industries, both in production processes, where the tools and machines with which work was carried out were transformed, and in products. But technological change never occurs in a social or organizational vacuum, and associated with this ramifying process of technological change were profound changes in the organization, content and management of work. There are many perspectives from which this historical change could be considered: in terms of the experience of the new working class, in terms of the role of women's and children's labour, in terms of its medical and social effects and so on.[1] However, these important issues will not be addressed here. I shall examine not the specific effects of changing work patterns, but

---

[1]   For some examples of these approaches, see I. Pinchbeck, *Women Workers and the Industrial Revolution 1750–1850* (London, 1981); M. Berg, *The Age of Manufactures 1700–1820* (London, 1985); E. P. Thompson, *The Making of the English Working Class* (Harmondsworth, 1984).

rather an important – but somewhat neglected – analytical and historical question: what were the causal links between technological change, industrialization and the changing nature of work? It is aspects of this question which will be discussed in this chapter, which examines the broad historical contours of change in work, and relates these changes to innovation and economic growth.

The historiographical background

There have always been those who offer an essentially technical–determinist answer to the above question: for them industrialization, with its new workplaces and forms of work, was *caused* by the innovation of new machines. In the first systematic work on British industrialization,[2] Arnold Toynbee argued for example that British economic growth and change since 1760 was solely caused by four key innovations in textiles, and by the innovation of a new power technology, Watt's steam engine: 'we find,' remarked Toynbee, 'the all-prominent fact to be the substitution of the factory for the domestic system, *the consequence of the mechanical discoveries of the time*' (my emphasis) (p. 69). So Toynbee saw the new social organization of work, of which the factory is the site and the symbol, as a result of technological innovation. Subsequent economic histories have rarely been as explicitly determinist as Toynbee, yet the emphasis which he placed on process innovations in equipment has frequently been followed by other historians, both of Britain and continental Europe.[3] Technological change, in this perspective, is seen largely as a matter of external changes in 'hardware', which then produced effects on output levels, production organization, work and the social system in general. Thus, in the view of one of the foremost historians of European technological development, David Landes, the new factory system of production was 'compelled' by developments in machinery.[4] This approach obscures, unfortunately, questions about how the new working relationships implied by the factory themselves affected and shaped the course, nature and rate of technological change.

[2]   A. Toynbee, *Lectures on the Industrial Revolution of the Eighteenth Century in England* (London, 1908).
[3]   For some examples of this see K. Bruland and K. Smith, 'Industrialization, steam power and economic historiography', *Economy and Society*, 10:1 (1981), p. 92.
[4]   D. Landes, *The Unbound Prometheus. Technological Change 1750 to the Present* (London, 1978), p. 81.

When technical change is seen as exogenous to the process of work and management, workers are in consequence usually seen as rather passive recipients of the effects of change. Thus, many historians have focused their attention on the impact of technological change on workers, rather than on the important shaping role which workers themselves played in determining the course of technical change. This emphasis derives, in large part, from some of the major nineteenth-century sources of our knowledge about industrialization and working life. For Britain, the most important of these were the substantial published reports of parliamentary committees on various aspects of industrialization: these reports were based on official hearings, taking a wide range of evidence on the impact of child labour, the moral and health effects of factory work, and so on. Similar investigations produced similar reports in many European countries.[5] Associated with these reports in Britain were profoundly influential commentaries, such as Charles Wing's *Evils of the Factory System*, James Kay-Shuttleworth's *Moral and Physical Condition of the Working Classes Employed in Manchester*, C. T. Thackrah's *Effects of Arts, Trades and Professions on Health and Longevity*, and John Fielden's *Curse of the Factory System*. All of these works were published in the 1830s, some based heavily on evidence to parliamentary committees, and all played an important part in focusing on the impact of technological change on workers rather than on their role in its causes or direction. Such works had a significant influence on the interpretations of industrialization which were developed in nineteenth-century western Europe. It was presumably these background themes, also, which shaped perhaps the most wide-ranging British historical debate on industrialization and the workers. This debate – which still continues – was over whether the impact of industrialization was to raise or lower their 'standard of living'; the debate has extended elsewhere in Europe.[6] Once again, workers and the working class have been seen essentially as simply recipients of the impact of technological change and industrialization, with the debate

[5]   Selections from a range of these continental reports are reproduced in S. Pollard and C. Holmes (eds), *Documents of European Economic History. Vol. I: The Process of Industrialization 1750–1870* (London, 1968).

[6]   An account of the British debate can be found in A. J. Taylor (ed.), *The Standard of Living in Britain in the Industrial Revolution* (London, 1975); for Germany see J. J. Lee, 'Labour in German industrialization', in: P. Mathias and M. Postan (eds), *Cambridge Economic History of Europe, Vol. VII, The Industrial Economies: Capital Labour and Enterprise. Part I* (Cambridge, 1978), pp. 471–4; for Scandinavia see *Scandinavian Economic History Review*. Special issue on the standard of living in Scandinavia, 34:2 (1986).

concentrating principally on one dimension of their working lives, namely real incomes.

There are two key problems with such perspectives, and therefore with much of the existing literature. The first is that it either obscures or gives us no coherent explanation of why technological change occurred, historically. Clearly, during the nineteenth century, Europe underwent an economic transition of great historical significance; economic systems emerged in which, for the first time in human history, technological change and productivity growth were rapid and continuous. Why did this happen? What was it about the European economic and production environment which elicited and sustained technological change? In particular, what role did changes in the organization and nature of work play in the acceleration of technological change from the late eighteenth century? The second problem in the perspectives described above is that they overstate the role of 'hardware' innovation, or tangible innovations in machinery, in European growth in the nineteenth century. In terms of equipment, many industries in nineteenth-century Europe deployed techniques which were continuations or adaptions of techniques used over a period stretching back to much earlier times. The 'revolutionary' impact of technological change in European industrialization was relatively small. It is important to note that the growth of industrial employment was not accompanied by a corresponding growth of mechanization. For Britain, 'the typical worker in the mid-nineteenth century was not a machine operator in a factory but still a traditional craftsman or labourer'[7] and Crafts has estimated that at most 19 per cent of workers were working in mechanized industry in 1841.[8] In the rest of Europe the development of mechanized factories was correspondingly slower. Ashworth notes that 'as late as 1834 there were still twice as many hand-looms as power-looms in the British cotton industry' and that, apart from Belgium, 'continental Europe had little mechanized industry to show' as late as 1850.[9] In early nineteenth-century Europe, therefore, 'industrial work' meant a variety of things; the modern mechanized factory was only one type of organization and coexisted with domestic labour, putting out, artisan workshops, the centralized manufactory and other forms of organization, some based on compulsory labour. Braudel argues:

[7]   A. E. Musson, *The Growth of British Industry* (London, 1978), p. 141, quoted in N. F. R. Crafts, *British Economic Growth during the Industrial Revolution* (Oxford, 1985), p. 8.
[8]   Crafts, *British Economic Growth*, p. 8.
[9]   W. Ashworth, *A Short History of the International Economy since 1850*, 4th edn (London, 1987), pp. 7–8, 11.

The bulk of pre-industry took the form of the many elementary units of craft production ... But above these dispersed workshops, there were already emerging enterprises of a frankly capitalist nature, the *manufactories* and the *factories* ... But, and this was a rule virtually without exceptions, manufactories always employed, beside their concentrated labour-force, out-workers in the town or the nearby countryside, all working at home.[10]

Understanding the role of change in the organization of production, and hence in the organization and experience of work, is central to both of the analytical and historical questions I have posed above. In what follows, I want to suggest two main arguments about the relation between changing work organization, technological innovation and economic growth.

Firstly, the process of industrialization was made possible by a changed organization of production: changes in control, managerial oversight and an increasingly sub-divided technical division of labour were the most important elements of this. It was not just that this provided the basis for subsequent technological change: it *was* technological change, for even without changes in tools and equipment, changes in methods ought to be considered as technological change. Thus, despite the non-mechanization of much of European industry, despite its apparent continuity in terms of technique, a process of significant technological change was going on within it. At the same time, however, it was these changes in methods, management and the character of work which made innovations in technical equipment possible. Changes in work were a necessary precondition for accelerated technological change.

Secondly, the response of workers to the impact of new organizations and new managerial imperatives was itself a major determining factor in shaping the direction of technological change. Sometimes this was a matter of a direct relation between labour conflict and innovation: managers and entrepreneurs tried to innovate or automate in such a way as to destroy the ability of workers to enforce high wages or to control production. More generally, new technologies always involved problems of labour management, and this affected those technologies which were in practice innovated.

Following sections will describe some historical examples of these processes, looking first at organizational change, work transformation

[10]   F. Braudel, *The Wheels of Commerce* (London, 1982), pp. 329–30. Examples and an account of this complex coexistence of different production forms can be found in P. Kriedte, H. Medick and J. Schlumbohm, *Industrialization before Industrialization* (Paris and Cambridge, 1981).

and economic growth, then at the relation between work organization and technological change.

Changing forms of production and work

Manufacturing production began, slowly, to be mechanized in Britain from the late eighteenth century. The rest of Europe lagged, but followed the British lead. From 1840 the whole of western Europe and large parts of eastern Europe were engaged in a full-scale transition to mechanized factory production in manufacturing. This dramatic change has obscured an equally dramatic, but less tangible change which preceded nineteenth-century industrialization: a large-scale transformation, over a long time period, in methods, organization and control of work. Limitations of space mean that the nature of this change can only be outlined here; this section simply gives some examples to indicate the structure of the development.

The central feature of pre-industrial production was that technological knowledge took the form of craft skills, and that those who possessed these skills controlled production processes. To 'control' in this context means to be able to determine the length of the working day, the intensity of work, the sequence of operations in production, and so on. This applied whether workers were employed on their own account, as individual artisans, or in workshops or early manufactories. What kind of work system prevailed when artisans themselves controlled output? E. P. Thompson has argued that the characteristic pattern was for 'alternate bouts of intense labour and idleness wherever men were in control of their working lives.'[11] In considering the amount of work that was actually done, Braudel suggests: 'We might bear in mind Vauban's calculation that the artisan worked 120 days per annum: holidays (there were plenty of these) and seasonal tasks swallowed up the rest of the year.'[12] This was not just a matter of cottage-based artisans:

> That a man could control his own work pace when working in his cottage is evident, but the pattern was also characteristic of the small workshops, where men paid by the piece came and went with an irregularity which did not pose too many problems for employers with little investment in fixed capital.[13]

[11] E. P. Thompson, 'Time, work discipline and industrial capitalism', in: M. W. Flinn and T. C. Smout (eds), *Essays in Social History* (London, 1974), p. 45.

[12] Braudel, *The Wheels of Commerce*, p. 306.

[13] J. Rule, *The Experience of Labour in Eighteenth-Century Industry* (London, 1981), p. 55.

In his investigations into the conditions of the working classes in France, Villerme drew attention to this difference between factory and workshop weaving: 'As for the workshop, where work is performed by hand, as the looms work without the help of motive power, and as wages are paid by the piece or the *aune*, hours are more flexible than is the case in other establishments.'[14] Mantoux quotes from a parliamentary report on children's employment, pointing out that the spinners who worked at home with the jenny or the mule 'frequently spent two or three days in the week in idleness and drinking, while the children they employed were often waiting on them at the public houses, till they were disposed to go to their work; and when they did go they continued it sometimes almost night and day.'[15]

In industries such as spinning, weaving, pottery, mining and the metal trades, workers so rarely worked on Mondays that it became known as 'St Monday'. Other industries had their characteristic saints' names for their 'holy days': shoemakers had St Crispin; smiths had St Clement; woolcombers had St Blaise.[16] This kind of production system had obvious inefficiencies, and there was clearly scope for costs to be cut and profits raised if entrepreneurs could find a way of exerting control of the intensity and duration of work.

Let me now describe a famous example of a case in which the above types of system were revolutionized into an organization of an essentially modern form, *without fundamental changes in technique*. The example is that of the English pottery master Josiah Wedgwood, whose operations came to dominate the English pottery industry, located in and around Stoke-on-Trent. The area remains an important pottery and ceramic production area, and the Wedgwood firm still exists today. How did Wedgwood establish his pre-eminence? In part this was due to great skill in marketing, but he managed to combine this with a radical transformation of production methods. I do not want to suggest that what Wedgwood did is directly typical of pre-industrial and industrial work transformation; but I do suggest that the structure of the change he initiated can be found very widely, and exemplifies a general long-term structural change in European work organization.

The work patterns described above were essentially the labour situation which Wedgwood found in the pottery industry. From the late

[14]   Quoted in Pollard and Holmes, *Documents of European Economic History*, p. 493.
[15]   P. Mantoux, *The Industrial Revolution in the Eighteenth Century* (London, 1964), p. 419.
[16]   Rule, *The Experience of Labour*, p. 207.

eighteenth century the industry had responded to increased demand for pottery wares with a shift from the family craftsman stage to a system based on 'the master potter with his journeymen and apprentices recruited from outside his family.'[17] But the system still relied on the working rhythms and working methods of the skilled potter:

> The stoppages for a wake or a fair or a three-day drinking spree were an accepted part of a potter's life – and they proved the most difficult to uproot. When they did work, they worked by rule of thumb; their methods of production were careless and uneconomical; and their working arrangements arbitrary, slipshod and unscientific. For they regarded the dirt, the inefficiency and the inevitable waste, which their methods involved, as the natural companions to pot-making.[18]

Wedgwood changed all this, and his work became 'a model' to the pottery industry, even though he was not helped by any 'startling mechanical invention'.[19] On the contrary he shared the basic techniques of the industry with his competitors. As noted above, his success owed much to product innovation and marketing, but his marketing strategy required implementation through new methods of management. In this the labour process was central: 'Having designed his system, Wedgwood had to train men to fit it, and to regiment them to exploit its potential.'[20]

The key elements of this new system were: (1) subdivision of tasks; (2) recruitment and training of new workers; and (3) work discipline.

Task subdivision Wedgwood's production was broken up into a long series of minor operations, each operation carried out by a specialized worker.

> The gradual multiplication of the processes whereby ceramic products could be produced led, as in other industries, to a marked division of labour. Josiah Wedgwood's Etruria, where the principle of specialization was first introduced, was divided into departments according to the type of ware produced: useful, ornamental, jasper, basalt, and so on. In 1790 some 160 employees were engaged in the 'useful' branch, in the following categories: slip-house, clay-beaters, throwers and their attendant boys, plate makers, dish makers, hollow-ware pressers, turners of flat ware, turners of hollow-ware, handlers, biscuit-oven firemen, dippers, brushers, placers and firemen in the glost

17   N. McKendrick, 'Josiah Wedgwood and factory discipline', *Historical Journal*, 4:1 (1961), p. 31. Reproduced by kind permission.
18   Ibid., p. 38.
19   S. Pollard, *The Genesis of Modern Management* (London, 1965), p. 265.
20   McKendrick, 'Josiah Wedgwood', p. 34.

oven, girl colour-grinders, painters, enamellers and gilders, and, in addition, coal getters, modellers, mould makers, saggar makers, and a cooper.[21]

From a technical point of view the increased division of labour implied the substitution of homogeneous for heterogeneous work; work consisting of repetition of similar tasks, rather than tasks proceeding vertically. Each operation was carried out in separate units by specialized workers: 'The same hands cannot make *fine, & coarse – expensive & cheap* articles.'[22]

Recruitment and training This new system first of all required a workforce equipped with the appropriate skills – as defined by Wedgwood. These were not readily available, and Wedgwood was compelled to secure his supply through training his own workers. This involved creating a labour force whose skills were limited to a narrower field – as a consequence of specialization – than hitherto common. Whether or not this was tantamount to de-skilling is very much a matter of definition; the craft aspect became less apparent, but at Wedgwood's, 'division of labour did not destroy skill: it limited its field of expression to a particular task, but within those limits it increased it.'[23] But it is important to note that Wedgwood controlled the production of skill, and he required workers who were willing to train on his terms. In the production of skills Wedgwood applied aspects of the old apprenticeship system, but he could suit it to his needs – sometimes insisting on his workers going through more than one apprenticeship as changing demands required changing skills. Thus the economic and social character of such training was transformed, and this transformation was intimately connected with the development of management.

Work discipline The worker not only had to acquire the new skills, but also be willing to work in a new way, in which the control of the period of work and the execution of work were increasingly in the hands of the employer. Working for Wedgwood meant, for most, working for a wage, rather than being paid by the piece. This system of pay was intimately linked to the centralizing of the management of production. How did the system of pay affect efficiency? The increasing division of labour had made it easier to specify the cost of labour more precisely, and 'to purchase exactly that precise quantity ... which is necessary for each process.'[24] This, 'Babbage's great principle of economical production', as

---

[21]   A. Clow and N. Clow, 'Ceramics from the fifteenth century to the rise of the Staffordshire potteries', in: C. Singer et al., *A History of Technology. Vol. IV: The Industrial Revolution c. 1750–c. 1850* (Oxford, 1958), p. 356–7.
[22]   McKendrick, 'Josiah Wedgwood', p. 32.
[23]   Ibid., p. 33.
[24]   Charles Babbage, quoted in H. Braverman, *Labour and Monopoly Capital* (New York, 1974), p. 80.

Alfred Marshall referred to it, led to savings in production costs and was important both in payment by piece and in wage payment systems. At Wedgwood's, 'the division of skills had crystallized into a settled factory strata', a 'fixed hierarchy' with weekly wages in the early 1790s ranging from 42s. to 1s.[25] But in order to realize the commercial benefits of this system, it was necessary that punctuality, duration of work and intensity of work be controlled. So in the first place, Wedgwood's workers were required to be punctual:

> ... workmen were summoned by ringing a bell ... the first warning at '1/4 of an hour before [the men] can see to work', again at 8.30 for breakfast, at nine to recall them and so on until 'the last bell when they can no longer see'.[26]

The period of work was determined by Wedgwood – rather than by the workers themselves – and he sought to enforce a regular working day also by means of the wage system. He employed a clerk whose instructions included:

> Those who come later than the hour appointed should be noticed, and if after repeated marks of disapprobation they do not come in due time, an account of the time they are deficient in should be taken, & *so much of their wages stopt* as the time comes to.[27]

Finally the content and character of work were defined and enforced: 'His workmen were not allowed to wander at will from one task to another as the workmen did in the pre-Wedgwood potteries. They were trained to one task and they had to stick to it.'[28] In order to enforce this new regime of work, Wedgwood gradually evolved a three-part disciplinary system comprising a formal structure of rules for the conduct of work and the operation of the plant (covering methods, use of materials, cleanliness and so on), a system of fines and penalties for infringements, and a supervisory system of overseers and inspectors (themselves hierarchically organized). Finally, the whole system was incorporated into a new plant layout, whose design was determined by the concern for ease of transport of input and output, efficient use of materials and by the structure of the new technical division of labour.

25   McKendrick, 'Josiah Wedgwood', p. 33.
26   Ibid., pp. 40–1.
27   Ibid., p. 41.
28   Ibid., p. 32.

The Wedgwood example is a justly famous one, for it incorporates many themes of industrial transformation, in particular the role of the vigorous, driven, far-sighted and determined entrepreneur. But it also suggests, in a particularly clear-cut way, the manner in which purely managerial and organizational transformations – directed primarily at the content, pace and duration of work – could produce growth in output and productivity, falling costs of production, and changes in industry structure. It would be wrong to suggest that the Wedgwood example was a typical one in terms of the clearness of its goals and the rapidity of its execution. Nevertheless, the overall process of change which it implies was very widespread; it occurred in many industries, over a longer time-scale, with less clarity in terms of objectives and greater confusion in terms of methods. But such change occurred nonetheless. It was, for example, a key element in so-called 'proto-industrialization' processes. And similar forms of change can readily be found, in similar industries, in different countries. For example, in their comparative study of Sir Robert Peel and C-P Oberkampf, the two most successful eighteenth-century textile printers in England and France, Chapman and Chassagne point out that,

> Both were martinets who used their considerable organising powers in rural areas to create a corps of disciplined and loyal workers, officers, NCOs, men, women and juveniles, all inured to the system. Contemporaries like Arkwright, Wedgwood and Marshall in England, and Richard-Lenoir, Koechlin and Perier in France, may have had an equal reputation, but none ruled with greater personal authority.[29]

This 'authority' was used to enforce new patterns of work. It is certainly possible to suggest, therefore, that the basic economic development in eighteenth and early nineteenth century Europe was change in the organization, and control of work at the level of the enterprise.

This large scale historical change had two significant consequences. On the one hand it led directly to economic growth. On the other, it established a production system in which technological change could occur. For entrepreneurs, it was a relatively short step from changing the technical division of labour and the control of work to seeking to change the instruments of work: seeking, that is, to make innovations in equipment. Changing the nature of work in the enterprise was the single most important pre-condition for this. Why was this?

At this point we should return to the questions with which this chapter

---

[29]   S. D. Chapman and S. Chassagne, *European Textile Printers in the Eighteenth Century. A Study of Peel and Oberkampf* (London, 1981), p. 209.

began. What is the relationship between changing work patterns, technological change and industrialization? In particular, (1) what was it about the European economic environment which encouraged technical innovation; and (2) how can we account for economic growth when 'hardware' innovation and mechanization were confined to so few industries? This section explores some tentative answers; specifically they suggest that the changing character of work was central to the overall process. It was the long historical process through which entrepreneurs gradually removed control of the production process from the individual craftsman or artisan which opened up the possibility of technical innovation and mechanical methods. This is because, from a technical point of view, it gave entrepreneurs a control of the overall production process which made it possible to envisage and install mechanical innovations; and from an economic point of view, the fact that entrepreneurs could appropriate the economic benefits – in the form of increased profits – gave them a powerful incentive to seek innovations. At the same time, these new work systems directly led to growth in output, productivity and incomes, and this enables us to understand why, even with mechanization limited in scope and application, European economic growth accelerated from the late eighteenth century. It was because, behind the apparent continuity in physical techniques, there was organizational innovation of a very radical kind. There was a fairly direct international diffusion of these changes from Britain, the originating economy: British workers, in most parts of Europe, played a significant role in spreading the new work systems, in training local workers, and in the adaptation of the workforce to the new rhythms of work.

Workers and the shaping of technological change

I have suggested above that the new work disciplines of the eighteenth and nineteenth centuries are central to the understanding of European economic growth. But these disciplines were not installed without a struggle. Workers actively or passively resisted, or otherwise attempted to modify, the new production system, and this had important implications for the evolution of technology itself.

Firstly, the new forms of enterprise had enormous difficulties simply in recruiting a labour force. The economic advantage of the new system, though definite, was often marginal, and where this left the possibility of alternative employment to workers they were eager to exploit that possibility. Jurgen Schlumbohm has pointed out that

The producers forcefully resisted . . . the shift of work from their homes to a location under the direct control of the entrepreneur. For as long as they continued to hope that their distressed conditions might improve, they tried to avoid this step and survive by other means. When some of them had from necessity taken it, the others often enough tried to defend their existence . . . through protests and even physical violence against the large workshops.[30]

Accepting a place in the new type of workshop or factory was, as the above section has suggested, to enter a radically different system:

The worker who left the background of his domestic workshop or peasant holding for the factory entered a new culture as well as a new sense of direction. It was not only that 'the new economic order needed . . . part humans: soulless, depersonalised, disembodied, who could become members, or little wheels rather, of a complex mechanism'. It was also that men who were non-accumulative, accustomed to work for subsistence . . . had to be made obedient to the cash stimulus, and obedient in such a way as to react precisely to the stimulus provided.[31]

Problems of recruitment led to a range of solutions on the part of early entrepreneurs: sub-contracting, for example, was extremely common – entrepreneurs would hire specialist workmen who would recruit and supervise ancillary labour which would often come from members of their own family). In many industries, and many countries, coercion was used: orphan children, prisoners, the destitute would be compelled to work in the new factories.[32] In Britain, for example, between 1790 and 1812, the important textile entrepreneur Samuel Oldknow obtained pauper apprentices from distant areas: among other places, from Ashford in Kent, from the London parish of Clerkenwell, and from London's Foundling Hospital.[33] At the same time, skilled workers were in short supply. These workers were not so concerned to avoid the factory since the factory was the main market for their skills, but they were always ready to move, and labour turnover was usually high. One of the largest Manchester cotton spinning firms, McConnell and Kennedy, had an average labour turnover in the early nineteenth century of 100 per cent per year, a high but not uncommon rate.[34] In Germany, employers 'were

---

[30]　Kriedte et al., *Industrialization before Industrialization*, pp. 108–9.
[31]　Pollard, *Genesis of Modern Management*, p. 161.
[32]　Ibid., pp. 162–5.
[33]　G. Unwin et al., *Samuel Oldknow* (London, 1924), p. 171.
[34]　Pollard, *Genesis of Modern Management*, p. 182; cf. R. Fitton and A. Wadsworth, *The Strutts and the Arkwrights 1758–1830* (Manchester, 1958), ch. 9.

generally satisfied if they achieved partial success in creating a stable core of skilled workers. . . . Turnover was the most persistent labour problem confronting employers.'[35] This situation gave immense bargaining strength to skilled workers in European industrialization, which they used to raise wages and dictate the pace of production.

One way in which entrepreneurs responded to this was by seeking technological developments which would diminish the skill requirements of the labour force. The most obvious historical examples of this can be found where strikes or labour conflict actually precipitated definite innovations. A famous discussion of this occurs in the work of Andrew Ure, who remarked in 1835 that 'when capital enlists science in her service, the refractory hand of labour will always be taught docility.'[36] Ure gives four examples of innovations in the textile industry generated by labour conflict: the first automatic cotton spinning machine (Richard Roberts's 'self-acting mule'); multi-colour textile printing machines; dyeing and rinsing machinery; and preparatory equipment in weaving.[37] In the spinning industry, Ure argued, the skilled spinners had

> . . . abused their powers beyond endurance, domineering in the most arrogant manner . . . over their masters. High wages, instead of leading to thankfulness of temper and improvement of mind, have, in too many cases, cherished pride and supplied funds for supporting refractory spirits in strikes.[38]

This led to an approach by spinning capitalists to the famous engineer Richard Roberts, who indeed solved their problem, developing the world's first complex automatic machine. One contemporary commentator remarked in 1835 that

> One of the recommendations of this machine to the spinners [that is the cotton entrepreneurs] is, that it renders them independent of the working spinners, whose combinations and stoppages of work have often been extremely annoying to the masters.[39]

---

[35]   J. J. Lee, 'Labour in German industrialization', in: P. Mathias and M. Postan (eds), *Cambridge Economic History of Europe, Vol. VII. The Industrial Economies: Capital Labour and Enterprise. Part I* (Cambridge, 1978), p. 460.
[36]   A. Ure, *The Philosophy of Manufactures* (London, 1967), p. 365.
[37]   A similar account can be found in S. Smiles, *Industrial Biography: Iron Workers and Tool Makers* (London, 1863).
[38]   Ure, *Philosophy of Manufactures*, pp. 366–7.
[39]   E. Baines, *History of the Cotton Manufacture in Great Britain* (London, 1966), p. 208.

In other words, Roberts had opened up the possibility of 'innovating around' the problem of skilled labour and labour conflict. Cotton entrepreneurs no longer depended upon skilled spinners, and could think in terms of a wider, cheaper and more docile workforce. Other examples of this particular impulse to innovation can easily be found. In fact the conflict–innovation relation can be demonstrated for a wide range of technologies in various industries, and is therefore an important component of any general account of the shaping of innovation patterns.[40] It is therefore possible to show a direct link between the world of work and the technological trajectory of the modern world. Marx was right to suggest that 'it would be possible to write a whole history of the inventions made since 1830 for the sole purpose of providing capital with weapons against working class revolt,' although it needs to be remembered that this is but one element shaping the course of technological change.

But it was not simply these direct relationships between work, conflict and innovation which had a shaping effect on modern technology. The transition in work organization, which I have described above, led to new elements entering the innovation decisions of firms. The new imperatives of the management of work meant that in the search for new technologies, and in the choice of techniques, managers and entrepreneurs always had to bear in mind the labour implications of any technical innovation. What kind of labour did it employ? How expensive was that labour? How skilled? What kind of control would it be able to exert over the pace and intensity of production? From the period when technological innovation began to accelerate, in the late eighteenth century, such questions became an integral part of the innovation decision in capitalist economies, and to some extent, therefore, the imperatives of work came to play a role in all technological change.

Conclusion

I have argued in this chapter that changes in labour organization and the character of work were important causal pre-conditions for the technolo-

---

[40]   For specific historical examples see K. Bruland, 'Industrial conflict as a source of technical innovation: three cases', *Economy and Society*, 11:2 (1982), pp. 91–121; R. Church, 'Problems and perspectives', in R. Church (ed.), *The Dynamics of Victorian Business* (London, 1980), p. 17; N. Rosenberg, 'The direction of technological change: inducement mechanisms and focusing devices', in: *Perspectives on Technology* (Cambridge, 1977).

gical changes which we normally associate with industrialization. Of course this does not mean that they were the only pre-conditions. European industrialization involved the intricate coalescence of many factors: scientific, legal, political and military influences all came together, and it would be wrong to argue that any of them had causal primacy. But the complex changes in the structure and organization of work and production, which have been described in these pages, also have their place. Neglect of their role in the causation and shaping of industrialization would be unjustified.

Notes on Contributors

T. C. Barker is Professor Emeritus of Economic History at the University of London.

Kristine Bruland is a fellow of the Centre for Technology and Culture at the University of Oslo and author of *British Technology and European Industrialization* (Cambridge University Press, 1989).

Nick Crafts is Professor of Economic History at the University of Warwick and formerly a fellow of University College, Oxford. He is author of *British Economic Growth During the Industrial Revolution* (Clarendon Press, 1985).

John A. Davis is chairman of the Centre for Social History and reader in modern history at the University of Warwick.

Peter Mathias was formerly Chichele Professor of Economic History at Oxford and is now Master of Downing College, Cambridge. He is the author of *The First Industrial Nation* (London, 1983).

Robert Woods is Professor of Geography and Director of the Graduate Programme in Population Studies at the University of Liverpool.

Index